SHREWSBURY

A Biography

The World within the Town

What would life in Shrewsbury have been like when the Anglo-Saxon King Aethelred held his Christmas feast here, or when the Norman conquerors enforced their power? How would King Henry IV's preparations for the battle at Shrewsbury have affected life within the town walls, or how did King Charles I vie for the inhabitants' hearts and minds during the Civil War?

These are just some of the questions this brief biography of Shrewsbury attempts to answer. It will also show that a town does not exist in isolation. It exists in relation to events played out on the larger historical canvas and sometimes it may even, involuntarily, become a major player.

'Shrewsbury - A Biography' is based on twelve articles first published in the *Shrewsbury Chronicle* during the autumn of 1999 as part of the Millennium celebrations.

Published by MPR Publishing Services Ltd.
PO Box 533, Shrewsbury SY3 8WY, UK
Email: *shrewsbury.biography@btinternet.com*

ISBN: 0-948579-13-7

Printed by Livesey Limited, Shrewsbury, UK

To my mother

Acknowledgements

I would like to thank my son Nick and my husband Bernard for their invaluable help in the production of this book. Thanks also to the *Shrewsbury Chronicle*, in particular to the editor John Butterworth, for his help and enthusiastic support for the project. I would like to thank Peter Holgate for reading the proofs. I am indebted to Mike Stokes and Mary White at the *Shrewsbury Museum and Art Gallery* for providing advice and many valuable pictures. Finally I would like to extend my thanks to Patricia Harris whose encouragement made me think about publishing the Millennium articles in book form in the first place.

The publisher also acknowledges the following for providing the images used in this book: Danny Beath, Mrs. Daphne Capps, Gordon Riley, Shropshire Records and Research Library, The Shropshire Archaeological Service, The Whitworth Art Gallery (University of Manchester) The Royal Archives, the British Museum, the John Rylands Library (University of Manchester), and the Shrewsbury Town Centre Management Partnership.

Contents

About the Author

Jrschina Williams-Karesch is a freelance historian/writer living in Shrewsbury. She has a BA in English and History and an MA in Modern European History from Birmingham University.

Preface

When first I came to Shrewsbury twenty-eight years ago I knew it only as a place where I was to change trains. I had left London and moved to Mid-Wales with my husband and young son to attempt the 'Good Life', like so many young and idealistic people during the 1970's.

Soon, however, we found that the blackberries we picked in the hedgerows didn't produce the clear wine we hoped for. The crop of potatoes on the little patch of earth proved a meagre one. The spinach had been nibbled to stalks by the snails and the carrots holed out by carrot flies. Tramping through the wet grass crossing the fields in my long London skirts (as was then the fashion) proved cumbersome as the wet robes clutched about my ankles and the cows, wide-eyed – surely laughed at me!

I began to realize then, that as much as I adored listening to the finches singing in the hedgerows in the morning, I also needed the facilities of a town. It was thus a compromise between the wild country and London that made us put our dice on Shrewsbury.

I have not regretted it. At that time many Londoners I knew regarded Shrewsbury as somewhere 'just beyond the edge of nowhere'. It has changed since then. It had never been a fair description anyway. Having been brought up in Switzerland, I thought that when I arrived in London this was England. After moving to Shrewsbury I realised that I was now learning about the real England.

As years went by, I frequently took visitors around the town. They perplexed me with questions such as 'Why did Charles I come to Shrewsbury? How? What did he do?' Questions I could not answer. It was to avoid further embarrassment, especially after I had acquired a degree in history, that I decided to read up about Charles I.

Subsequently I wrote an article, thinking perhaps someone else might want to know. I sent it to the Shrewsbury Chronicle. The response was rapid. John Butterworth, the Editor, called me into his office. It happened that the 2nd Millennium was just about to come to an end, and John said, 'What about...'

I have found that, no matter whether you study local history or world history, all things are connected. It is this connection between a place and the wider world that is to me the essence of any history. And it is this connection I have tried to emphasise in this short work.

Shrewsbury, February 2003

Chapter 1

Before the Fortress of Scrob
AD 67 - 900

Shrewsbury cannot look back upon a Roman pedigree. It has no coloured fragments of mosaic flooring. It has no stone slabs left scattered about from monumental arches or outlines of Roman baths. One may ponder the question why the Romans did not set foot here. Why they did not perceive the value of the natural defences offered by this knoll in the Severn loop so prized by later invaders?

The answer probably is geography. Romans did not like to build on hilly ground. They needed room for straight roads and expansive baths! The spot on which the town of Shrewsbury was to be established would not have suited them. It would have meant building in curves and angles.

Besides, the Roman military machine was so overwhelming that it did not require the help of nature. So when the first Roman legion foot-slogged its way towards Wales during the second century AD, its military strategists chose to build a military fort, which later became a town, five miles south-east from here. They called it Viroconium (today's Wroxeter).

Yet how can one know for sure whether some kind of settlement had, or had not, existed on the present Shrewsbury site before the Romans conquered Britain? A bronze axe hammer found during the 19th century on the site of today's High Street certainly points to an Iron Age settlement. A settlement perhaps which housed a tribal chief and his extended family. A colony of timber huts and pens for livestock may have existed during the early period of the Roman invasion. It may even have become a rebel stronghold for Cornovii (the name of the dominant local tribe at the time) freedom fighters. The Roman invasion had, after all, not been unopposed.

One cannot really know for sure. Timber huts, if there had been any, would have left little evidence behind. A rebel stronghold, by its very nature, hides its tracks. In either case, had such places existed, the Roman military would have made short shrift of them. It regarded tribal villages in naturally protected sites as potential breeding grounds for rebellion. For that reason it used to move people out of such areas into more easily controlled ones. Preferably, these people were relocated near one of the newly-established military towns. In this particular case they would have been moved to nearby Viroconium.

As for the period during Roman occupation, it is quite possible that Roman legionaries, when not compelled to practice stone-slinging, archery, swimming, riding or take part in mock battles at the Viroconium military camp, paddled upstream on the lovely River Severn. They may have landed on the spot of today's Shrewsbury for a little solitude and praised Sabrina, the Roman Goddess of the Severn. Maybe they relished an escape from the constant company of 5000 soldiers and 300 cavalry (the normal size of a Roman legion) the hustle and bustle of market traders, beerhouses and brothels. Many a Roman soldier may have sat here on the riverbank on a sunny summer's day, perhaps reciting Virgil, or met up with a local girl and dreamt of settling down.

Most Roman legionaries, on retirement from military service, settled down in the area in which they had served. Twenty-five years was the usual time of service, after which they were awarded either a choice of land, or a sum of money. Although initially Roman soldiers were not allowed to marry, this law had become obsolete by the end of the 2nd century AD.

To a local Cornovii girl, marriage to a Roman soldier would have been a 'brilliant match'. Quite apart from the strapping appearance of a soldier, bare legs, bright red tunic, crested helmet, it would have meant climbing the social ladder. For the Romans were considered to be the ruling elite. It would have meant status, wealth and guaranteed a substantial villa with thick stone walls and windows of glass. And a weekend villa upstream perhaps? Roman coins found near today's town centre suggest that some interaction between Viroconium and what today is the site of Shrewsbury had taken place....unless the coins had been pilfered by Anglo-Saxons and lost while pursuing their own business!

This is all speculation. One may never know. History is forever unfolding. The uncovering of the past is always ongoing. Who knows what may yet be found under the medieval foundations on which many later buildings have been constructed? Before the middle of the 19th century 'Viroconium' had been a field on which crops were sown and harvested for generations until some Victorian archaeologists spotted the signs and started to dig! Since then Roman helmet handles, lances, javelin tips and 'Hippo' sandals have been uncovered as well as mirror handles, spangles, spindles, statuettes of Venus, Diana and of Mercury, and Melon beads said to have been used as token of affection between Roman soldiers and local girls. [1]

As long as the Roman hold was strong, the various dynasties in this area, it seems, lived reasonably at peace with each other. Once the Roman Empire started to disintegrate a jostling for power began. (Perhaps not dissimilar to the 'tribal' wars in Yugoslavia following the collapse of the Eastern Bloc.)

By 400 AD and until approximately 600 AD, the most dominant dynasty was said to have been that of the Princes of Powys. Unlike the Romans, however, the Princes had no substantial army at their disposal. The natural defences offered by this knoll in the loop of the Severn would have seemed just perfect.

There has been speculation that the Princes of Powys made their Court at Shrewsbury and that at the time it was called Pengwern. The Princes of Powys were said to have held Pengwern until the Anglo-Saxons invaded Britain during the 7th and 8th century. This speculation is not undisputed. Poetry and myths lamenting the loss of Pengwern and the defeat of the Princes of Powys are the only sources available so far to throw some light on the subject.

Among the new Anglo-Saxon conquerors was the Mercian King Offa (King of the Midlands) who ruled from 755 – 795 AD. King Offa consolidated his realm by making peace with Wales. To ensure continuation of peace he had a great dyke built to draw a line between the two territories. This was an earthen wall 2 ½ metres high and up to 20 metres wide with a ditch alongside over a distance of 240 km from Prestatyn to Chepstow. Today much of it serves as a long distance footpath. King Offa's Dyke was almost a carbon copy of Hadrian's Wall built by the Romans five hundred years earlier to keep the 'Barbarians' out. The Barbarians to the Romans had been the Scots or anybody else who was not Romanised.

The Welsh who found themselves on the other side of Offa's Dyke did not readily accept this new border. They regarded themselves to be still proudly 'ancient, Romanised, Britons'. 'Welsh' according to the Welsh historian John Davies meant not 'foreigner' but rather 'people who had been Romanised'. These 'Welsh' spoke with contempt about the new rulers on the other side of the dyke. A Welsh (Romanised) poet described the Anglo-Saxons as 'these foreigners… so lacking in lineage'. The poet urged the Welsh, Irish and Northmen to unite to get these 'foreigners' out and into exile.

It was probably during the period of King Offa that one or two wooden churches were built on this knoll on which present-day Shrewsbury is situated. All the main churches in Shrewsbury are believed to have had their beginnings during the Anglo-Saxon period.

A bronze pin, which might have been used as a stylus or a girl's hairpin, is all the evidence there is of Shrewsbury's early Anglo-Saxon existence. The bronze pin[2], discovered on the site of what today is referred to as 'Old St. Chad's', is thought to date back to the 8th or 9th century. The Anglo-Saxon settlers, monks or prospectors, may have found virgin territory. They may have had to cut their way through brushwood and forest growth. On the other hand, they may have followed a trail once used by the Princes of Powys. They may even have built their churches with timber from the abandoned Court of the Princes.

If the new settlers hoped for peaceful times, their hopes were not fulfilled. Within a century, another wave of invaders, this time Danes and Vikings, as well as constant raids from the Welsh across the dyke, threatened their livelihood. It was because of these unsettling skirmishes that the then ruling monarch, King Alfred, in the year 870, ordered defences to be built around the newly established Anglo-Saxon settlements and Shrewsbury (Scrobbes-byrig) was 'officially' born.

The name of 'Scrobbes-byrig' appeared in a document in the year 901. The word of 'Scrob' puzzled historians and for a time it was interpreted as a reference to 'a place in the scrub'. In more recent times the interpretation has taken hold that it referred to a town named after a landowner called Scrob whose responsibility it had been to fortify the town. Scrobbes-byrig literally means the 'Fortress of Scrob'.

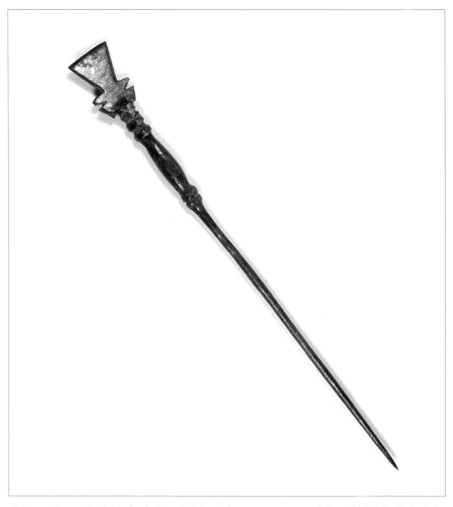

A bronze pin or stylus, believed to be from the 8th or 9th century, was excavated from Old St. Chad's site during the late 19th century. It is on display at Shrewsbury Museum & Art Gallery

St. Alkmund's Square, the original Anglo-Saxon Market Place.

Chapter 2

King Aethelred's Feast

1006

Thus writes a London scribe during the 11th century:

'In the year 1006 King Aethelred the Unready had gone across the Thames into Scrobbes-byrigscire to receive there his food-rent into the Christmas season'.

There was nothing unusual about the King travelling around his kingdom. Apart from collecting the food rents (taxes from subject people) and fines, it was important to be seen in order to remind everyone, especially the nobles, who was in control. Scrobbesbyrigscire (Shropshire) was a particularly volatile region and King Aethelred's position as monarch was shaky.

King Aethelred had unexpectedly acquired the crown as a child of ten in 978 after his mother had employed her own henchmen to have his older stepbrother murdered. 'Worse deed was never done among the English' recorded a scribe. The epithet 'unready' is derived from 'unraed', meaning 'evil counsel'.

At the time of his visit to Shropshire the King was thirty-eight years old. He had a reputation for double-dealing. He was unpredictable and cruel and he had an insatiable appetite for women. So some said!

Scrobbesbyrig by the year 1006 had become well established as a town and the capital of Scrobbesbyrigscire. It had a Shire-reeve (Sheriff), who was the King's representative. It had fortifications consisting of timber walls and earth ramparts. It had a watchtower, named 'Scrob's Tower' perhaps? The tower was strategically situated to guard the tongue of land where the Severn did not provide a natural defence. Today it is the site of the Castle.

Fortified Shrewsbury would not only have been valued by kings but by ordinary people. Life during the 11th century was as much fraught with insecurity as in previous centuries. Tribal disputes, personal vendettas, robber bands and raids by the Welsh made living dangerous, even more so in unprotected areas where villages were routinely burnt down. It was for that reason that during this period ordinary village people, small farmers and artisans, tended to seek protection under more powerful bodies. They either attached themselves and their family to the lord of a fortified manor or they sought shelter in a fortified town.

This protection, however, was at the expense of personal 'freedom'. People became 'villeins' or serfs committed to labour obligations. Most of Shrewsbury's inhabitants would at this time in some way or another have been attached to Church or King. There was only one way out of this. Trade! That was why one of the most important developments for Shrewsbury at this time was the Royal Permission to hold a weekly market and an annual fair.

St. Alkmund's Square used to be the Anglo-Saxon market place. Here once a week local people would display their home produce. Exchange eggs for bushels of peas. Fish for a loaf of bread. A reed basket for a new bridle. A hen for fixing a horseshoe. They would barter with the fishmonger, baker, butcher (flesh monger), all of whom could be found in every Anglo-Saxon town. They would exchange gossip over a cup of mead. They would ask, 'Have you seen Penny-Purse?' 'How is Soft-Bread today? Say, 'Come here Clean-Hand' or remark to a neighbour 'look Foul-Beard has drunk too much again'. People had no surnames then but addressed each other according to the jobs they did or other distinguishing characteristics.

In the market place locals mingled with the metal trader who delivered metal to the blacksmith. Without metal the blacksmith could not make helmets, spearheads, axes, knives or horseshoes. The wool fell trader brought essential raw material for the spinning of yarn to be made into cloth. The salt peddler delivered salt necessary to preserve fish and meat for the long winter months.

The most exciting event of the year was the Annual Fair held during the first three days in June. During these three days merchants who had travelled on horseback in caravans, who had braved waterlogged forest tracks (Forestels) and who had been prepared to face bears, wolves, wild boars and robbers to reach their chosen destination, displayed their wares. Spices from Jerusalem, gold rings from Arabia, silver goblets, jewellery, mirrors, silk-cloth. These merchants would have the manner and airs of a wider world - Burgundy, Venice, London.

Shrewsbury as it might have looked around 1100AD. Drawing by Peter Scholefield (by kind permission of the Shropshire Archaeology Service)

Shrewsbury's economic life, as shown by the many coins and fragments of crockery found here, was thriving during the 11th century. The tinkling of silver coins would have been a common sound. Shrewsbury had three moneyers. Moneyers were gold- or silversmiths by trade who had permission to press silver coins with a die supplied by the Royal Government. Coins would have been frequently used among Church, Court and local gentry but less frequently among the ordinary inhabitants. But trade, however limited in scale and in whatever 'currency' it was transacted, would have allowed a freedom unknown to most people living in the surrounding countryside.

Where there was money to be made, there were reeves. Reeves were tax collectors. Shrewsbury had several resident reeves. Taxes collected included market tolls and the obligatory 'tenth', the equivalent to today's income tax. Livestock, produce from the land, tools of the trade and any income derived from them were also taxed. Most families would have owned a pig or two, a few sheep and hens and everybody had access to common fields - The Common - where animals could graze. Most families would have had a patch of open ground to grow vegetables. The illustration on page 17 gives some idea of what Shrewsbury might have looked like around 1100.

Other taxes included the marriage tax. A widow, it is said, had to pay the King twenty shillings for a licence to marry. A maiden ten shillings. Marriage seems to have been for the better off.

The Shire-reeve was responsible for collecting the money from fines. Among the finable offences were: 'assault committed on the Forestel (Highway), ten shillings; refusal to accompany the King into Wales when residing in town, forty shillings; for a house burnt down 'accidentally without negligence', forty shillings.

The offence of house-fire was considered a severe one. Houses were of simple construction. They had timber or wattle walls and thatched roofs. They consisted of one room used by the whole family as well as some of the livestock. The earthen floor was strewn with rushes for warmth and comfort. In the middle of the room was an open fire that served both as heater and cooker. Fire was a constant hazard and the Royal income derived therefrom considerable.

Taxes could be paid in kind as well as in cash. King Aethelred's decision to collect his 'food-rents' himself would have meant that on his arrival bushels of peas, eggs and livestock would have been awaiting him in plenty as well as purses filled with coins.

The King was said to have had a residence in Shrewsbury. Perhaps it was called 'The Great Hall' and situated next to 'Scrob's Tower'. According to the scribe the King held a Christmas feast here in 'great state' in the company of all the invited nobles.

The scented smoke of roast swan and roast boar rising from the 'Great Hall's' chimneys may have brought the children out into the muddy lanes to taste the air with their tongues. They might not necessarily have gone without a feast themselves. Their parents may have slaughtered the summer-fattened pig. Yet overindulgence would not have been wise. A Royal visitor in town meant labour obligation. If the King wished to make a visit into Wales, some of the burgesses had to accompany him. Nobody wanted to have to pay a forty shillings fine.

In the year 1006 a Welsh trip was not planned. The King had opted for the 'Boxing Day Hunt' accompanied by his nobles only. The party set out to nearby Condover forest where, according to one of the nobles by the name of Henry of Huntington (he may himself have partaken in the Christmas feast and therefore have had first hand information) someone tried to murder the King.

Later it turned out to have been a plot hatched by a dissatisfied noble. This noble, so it was said, had contracted a Shrewsbury butcher named 'Porkhund' to commit the murder. The attempt was not successful. No one knows what happened to 'Porkhund' afterwards. However, as a consequence of the unfortunate incident, the King ordered the Shire-reeve to provide in future twelve of Shrewsbury's chief burgesses as guards 'whenever the King was engaged in the chase or during the King's residence in Shrewsbury'.

For Shrewsbury this marked the first step towards self-determination. To be elected to guard the King would have included permission to carry arms. A great honour at a time when the privilege was exclusively reserved for the nobility. But the King apparently trusted the burgesses more than the nobility. Future Town Corporations were to learn to exploit this 'Loyalty Card'.

However, it seems King Aethelred the Unready never managed to visit Shrewsbury again. He died in the year 1016. His reign was assessed as an inglorious one. His son, Edward the Confessor, although less flamboyant, was said to have been equally ineffective in controlling the realm. So preoccupied were the Anglo-Saxon warrior nobility with their own squabbles that they presented a weak front to any outsider hungry for territory.

On 14 October 1066 William of Normandy, subsequently known as William the Conqueror, landed with his army in England and defeated the Anglo-Saxon King Harold at Hastings.

At Shrewsbury, one Anglo-Saxon noble called Edrig the Wild of Herefordshire, tried to fight off the new arrivals in the year 1069. The defensive strike, in which many locals seemed to have been ready to assist, failed. By 1070 the Norman conquerors had almost complete control over England. Anglo-Saxon aristocratic families were removed from their estates to make room for the new order of nobles brought in by William.

Chapter 3

A Lucrative Investment

1070 - 1350

William the Conqueror ordered every item of property in his new realm to be counted and listed. The inventory, called the Domesday Book, shows that Shrewsbury at the time of the Conquest had 250 dwellings. If one counted six persons per dwelling the number of inhabitants would have been around 1,500.

As a symbol of new authority the ramshackle Anglo-Saxon watch tower, probably damaged during the last stand of Edrig the Wild, was replaced with a brand new one. It was whitewashed so that it could be seen from afar as well as look down upon the townspeople living under its shadow.

The Norman invasion was not only a military conquest. It was also a cultural one. Away went the old elite. In came the new. The Norman knights who had helped William win the battle of Hastings were rewarded with the estates which had belonged to the Anglo-Saxon nobles. The Earl of Montgomery, William's kinsman and companion in battle, was given Shrewsbury and, in addition, large chunks of Shropshire and Mid-Wales.

In the train of the Norman military had also come Norman merchants, traders, servants, craftsmen and artisans. Their intention was to settle here. Initial resentment against these 'cocky' newcomers, who spread themselves about as if they owned the place, may well have been high. The Norman Royal administration, however, left no doubt as to who was going to have the upper hand.

Discriminatory laws were introduced. The Normans did not have to pay taxes. The taxes of the English were doubled. The Murdrum law stated that any act of murder would be avenged on the whole community unless 'the dead was a mere Englishman'.

Among the first things the Earl of Montgomery did was to found the

The Tower situated on one of the highest points in Shrewsbury Castle grounds. Now named Laura's tower, it is built on the site of the original motte. From here the Anglo-Saxon noble Scrob, and later the Norman Earls of Montgomery, kept guard over the countryside and town. The tower as it stands today was built by Thomas Telford in the 1780's. (Photo: © Danny Beath).

Benedictine Abbey just outside Shrewsbury in the year 1083. The monks there were to pray for him - and take care of his conscience - while he would do the fighting. The Earl's reputation, as well as that of his kinsmen, was fierce but he was probably no worse than any other warlord of that period.

Medieval social hierarchy was divided into three tiers: 'Those who fight; those who pray; those who work'. And there was plenty of fighting still to do. Wales had never accepted Anglo-Saxon rule over its territory. It had no intention of accepting Norman rule now.

The borderlands between England and the as yet unconquered Wales William awarded to his most loyal commanders. These men were to be known as the Marcher Lords. The Earl of Mortimer and the Earl of Montgomery counted among them. The Marcher Lords were expected to keep the Welsh off the King's back. They had a licence to police this buffer zone at 'their discretion'. This licence was variably interpreted depending on the aggression vented from one side of the border or the other.

The Normans found the process of subduing the Welsh rather frustrating. The splendid castles of Caernarvon, Carmarthen, Beaulieu and Conway are living reminders of that period, when Norman dominance became imprinted in stone on the Welsh landscape.

As far as Shrewsbury was concerned, the Welsh wars were an advantage rather than a disadvantage, although initially they would not have been perceived as such. The local population was forced to build roads and bridges. The Welsh and English Bridges were both finished around 1100. The building of roads and bridges was primarily for the purpose of fighting the wars with Wales. However, the very same roads and bridges that brought armies to and from Wales also allowed easier access to Mid- and North Wales, London, Flanders and Normandy, which would have been to the great benefit of local wool and cloth merchants. It also seems that, with the Normans in control, travelling had become safer. A chronicler noted that 'now any man of substance could travel unmolested through the country with his bosom full of gold'.

As a frontier town, Shrewsbury became a centre for diplomatic activities. King Henry III, accompanied by his court, private army and papal officials, counted among the frequent visitors. The King came here to sign peace treaties, attend a parliament or consult with the Marcher Lords on war strategy. Shrewsbury was also the last town before entering the 'wilderness' of Wales. It was much appreciated by travellers. In 1188 the Archbishop of Canterbury among whose duties it was to excommunicate the Welsh rebels, praised 'Slopesbury' as a town which 'after the bleak and barren mountains of Wales was an oasis where one could refresh oneself and recruit new staff and horses'.

Despite the occasional attacks by Welsh rebel leaders - in the year 1215 the Welsh Prince Llewelyn took Shrewsbury Castle and occupied it for three months - Shrewsbury represented a safe haven, especially after the new town wall of solid stone had been built to protect the enlarged town area.

Over a century or so after the Normans' first arrival Shrewsbury had prospered and grown into one of the most important and richest towns in England. Forgotten were the early oppressions. Now inhabitants who wanted to be of consequence took on French airs. They addressed each other as Monsieur William de Burgg, Monsieur Nicholas de Bakelare, Monsieur Richard de Hulton. French was spoken to impress. The richer burgesses had wine, not ale or mead, with their dinner. And the rabbit, introduced by the Normans, may well have been served up as a latest food fad in the form of rabbit stew.

Kings, the nobility, ecclesiastics, merchants, traders, peddlers, monks, servants, soldiers, wives and daughters who accompanied their husbands or fathers during the meeting of the Royal Law Court would regularly rub shoulders with locals as they shopped and pursued their business in town. They would thread their way carefully through the narrow streets and lanes carpeted with horse manure, avoiding the kennel (the groove in the middle of the street carrying the slop and rainwater downhill). Roaming pigs, dogs, cats and chickens would occasionally bar their way. Or they might stop and watch a scene of execution, or a rebel found guilty being 'dragged at a horse's tail through the streets'.

Taverns and cook-shops would have done a roaring trade. So would the artisans and craftsmen in town as demand for leather gloves, fur rugs, silver buckles, spoons, silver brooches, cloth, parchment and spices increased. By the middle of the thirteenth century more than a dozen mercers had retail stores in town. There were a number of tailors, spicers, two apothecaries, harpers (musicians) and one dealer in parchment.

Increased demand for goods fuelled production of raw materials. The suburbs of Frankwell, Coleham and Castle Foregate developed. Here the skinners and tanners worked overtime to meet demands from town workshops. Lively and noisy places they would have been. The air filled with the ever pervading smell of leather being tanned.

Prosperity was followed by a building boom. The town's churches were rebuilt in stone. A Guildhall was built. Rich wool merchants now wanted houses with 'facilities', a kitchen with a baking oven. The ultimate status symbol was to have your own cesspit with an overlying garderobe. The less prosperous consoled themselves with new rushes on the floor, perhaps an upstairs room with a bed and a new straw mattress.

By the middle of the 13th century Shrewsbury numbered around 4,000 inhabitants. Many had been newcomers from the surrounding countryside. Usually these were young people starting to work as servants in burgess families or were apprenticed to a local craftsman. Moving into town was more than just an escape from home. It was a route to freedom, sometimes prosperity and burgess status. A burgess could own property or a plot of land. The route was open to anybody provided he (never a she) followed an honest trade.

Wealth and prosperity as well as loyalty made the King look upon Shrewsbury favourably as it brought substantial Royal tax revenue. As a result Shrewsbury Corporation had much muscle to ask for increasing self-determination in the affairs of the town. The Town Charter of 1226/7 shows how much political freedom had been gained over a century. It reads:

'None of the King's sheriffs shall intermeddle with the burgesses in any plea or quarrel'.

In other words, the power of the King's sheriffs had been curtailed.

'The said burgesses and their heirs may have a merchant guild with a Hansa and other customs and liberties belonging to such guild: and no one who does not belong to the Guild shall exercise merchandise in the borough without the consent of the burgesses'.

In other words, the local craftsmen were given the monopoly with members of the Guild to decide at their discretion who should be allowed to trade in the town.

'If any native or any person shall remain in the said Borough, and hold himself in the said guild, and in lot and scot with the said burgesses for one year and a day

The medieval Abbey of Shrewsbury founded by the first Earl of Montgomery. Only the parish church section remains today. The pulpit on the left is one of only three remaining in the country, and the only one in its original location. (Photo: © Danny Beath)

*without challenge (i.e. without being claimed by his lord): he may not be again
demanded by his lord if he freely continue in the said Borough'*

In other words a person who escaped his bondage and had been residence
in town for a year without causing trouble became a free person.

*'The burgesses of Shrewsbury and their heirs shall be free of pontage (a toll paid
for passing over a bridge); stallage (a duty paid for permission to set up stall in
market or fair); lene (to contribute to forced loans by kind); danegeld (land tax)
and all other customs and exactions, both in England and all other of the King's
territories, saving of London'.*

In other words, Shrewsbury merchants and traders were given generous
tax concessions.

Soon Shrewsbury was to have a representative in Parliament. The first in the
year 1268, the second in 1295. It thus felt doubly frustrating to the Town
Corporation, which included rich merchants such as the Roger Prides, the Richard
Borreys, the John Ludlows, that despite all the new power for self-determination
there was one body which consistently threw a spanner into their good work.
And this was the Abbey headed by the Abbot.

The Abbey community was a separate unit just outside the town. The
status of the Abbot equalled that of a feudal lord. It had grown in size and
power parallel to Shrewsbury during that period. The Abbey had, of course,
had a head start. Not only had it been richly endowed by the first Earl of
Montgomery but it had also been awarded the monopoly over the flourmills in
town. If there was one sure investment potential during the Middle Ages, apart
from founding a town on the right spot, it was flourmills, whether horse drawn
or wind powered. People always needed flour for bread.

The dispute over the mills was that, under the Grant of Foundation given by
Henry I, the monks of Shrewsbury, so they claimed, possessed the exclusive
privilege of grinding all the corn used in town and the sole right of owning mills
within its limits. The Town Corporation, however, claimed that Henry II had
given it the right to erect mills.

It was a long-winded dispute and it rankled deeply. The Corporation had, it
seemed, no document to prove Henry II's word – not uncommon during the

period. Should the Town Corporation idly look on whilst a potential income, that could be used to the benefit of the whole community, was being frittered away into some golden chest belonging to the Church? This was probably one of the questions they asked themselves. During that period the Church's flamboyance and open display of wealth had been frequently criticised as in no way conforming to the Christian message of humility it supposed to preach.

Perhaps this was one reason that induced the Town Corporation to invite (with permission of the King) the friars to set up their communities in Shrewsbury. Town parishes had always provided some charitable services, hospitals and schooling, but the friars' fundamentalist philosophy to live life according to the example of Christ created a sharp contrast to the established Church. The friars settled in the outskirts of town, cared for the poor and the lepers, and most of all, they offered cut-price baptisms and burials. They undercut the established Church.

It was during the second half of the 13th century that the dispute over the flour and water mills erupted into open hostility. The subject may have once again cropped up while pondering other matters. These included: the changing of the market place in order to have more space; a complaint arising from the paving of the High Street that the 'vast amount of evil-smelling mud formed on this new road surface did not disappear but lasted nearly the whole year round'; a complaint that the 'feckless carter with his overheavy loads and iron shod wheels made too much noise on the paved road'; the question of employing a constable and a rubbish carter; the supply of fresh water; a sewerage system.

Shrewsbury, it appears, had disregarded the Abbey monopoly. It had built three horse mills and one windmill. There may well have been more. Where they were positioned is not known. Probably both inside and outside the town wall. There were certainly some in the suburbs. Shrewsbury Town Corporation had also sought to cut out the competition from the Abbey altogether by preventing its own burgesses from using the Abbey mills.

The Abbot with his monks initially kept quiet. They seemed to have bided their time, and possibly for a while the groaning sound of the heaving wooden sails of the windmills cut the air peacefully enough. However, when it came to servicing the engines, the monks refused the town engineers access. Even worse the monks threatened to destroy the town's fishery nearby if anybody tried to service the illegally-erected mills.

The Abbot took the dispute to the King, now Henry III. The King paid little attention to Shrewsbury Town Corporation's claim that his predecessor Henry II had given permission to build the mills. Appeasement was called for. Arbitration was tried. The King wanted to remain in the good books of both parties. He needed the goodwill of Shrewsbury so that it would keep a careful eye on the Welsh. He also needed the goodwill of the Abbot whose power could not be ignored, especially as the Abbey was in possession of the bones of St. Winifred, which were believed to have supernatural power.

Nothing proved successful. Finally Henry III ordered that the flour mills in the suburbs should be destroyed and that those within the town should be maintained at the common expense of both parties. He also ordered that the two water mills applied for should be erected in the Severn at joint expense of Abbey and Town Corporation. And that the fishery of the burgesses was to be saved. A promise had to be made that in future no one would try to obstruct any person from repairing the Abbey Mills and that new mills, if necessary, should be common projects.

It was not until 1329, that the Town Corporation was at last permitted to erect its own 'engines'.

Butcher Row, Fish Street, Milk Street, Grope Lane with its overhanging roofs, Pride Hill, named after a rich wool merchant, are among the many reminders of medieval Shrewsbury. The Dominican Friary (Black Friars) sited near St. Mary's Water Lane has long disappeared. So has Austin (Augustinian) Friary on the site of Shrewsbury Sixth Form College, Welsh Bridge). The Franciscan Friary is still partly intact near Greyfriars Bridge (Coleham Footbridge).

Chapter 4

The Battle of Shrewsbury
1403

I t had been a long hot summer in the year 1403. The harvest of barley, oats and peas looked promising. No one could foresee that this promising harvest would be soaked with the blood of thousands of soldiers fighting a battle at Shrewsbury.

Part I – The King

It all had happened very quickly. On 12th July 1403 King Henry IV on his way to the Scottish border had just arrived at Nottingham when he heard rumours that a major rebellion was being staged on the Welsh border. As a precaution he decided to change course westwards with his small army. By the time he reached Burton-on-Trent the rumours were confirmed. Three armies were marching towards Shrewsbury (see map on page 32).

The three rebel armies were that of Percy 'Hotspur'; the Earl of Northumberland's army and the army of Owen Glyndwr, the Welsh leader, supported by the powerful Marcher Lord Mortimer and the Earl of Worcester.

But why did they march towards Shrewsbury? Why did they not confront the King in battle somewhere along his route northwards?

There could only have been one reason. Henry's fifteen-year-old son Harry (Hal), Prince of Wales, was staying at Shrewsbury. The Prince had been in the area for some time, entrusted to the Earl of Worcester, his uncle, to be tutored in the art of warfare. And now, after the Earl of Worcester had joined in the rebels' cause, the Prince was isolated here with only a small military guard.

Henry knew without a doubt that if the rebels captured the Prince of Wales at Shrewsbury they would hold him to ransom. If the rebels' demands were not met they would imprison or perhaps even kill him. Henry therefore had to

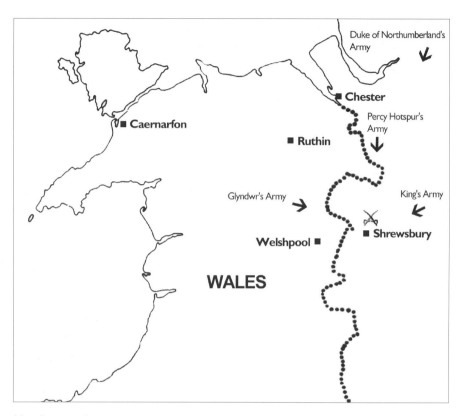

Map illustrating the armies marching towards Shrewsbury before the Battle.

decide quickly what to do. Should he wait until he had collected an army strong enough to crush the rebels? Percy's army was said to be 20,000 strong. Or should he hurry towards Shrewsbury with the small army at his disposal and take a chance?

To get a sufficiently powerful army together would take time. Foot soldiers were no problem. Gardeners, woodland labourers, field-hands keen for adventure and money, were easy to come by. As for equipment, they would bring with them the tools of their trade, pickaxes, shovels, bows and arrows.

Getting knights with fully equipped war-horses was a longer process. The war-horse, bred over centuries into a powerful war machine, needed the latest stirrups, a high back saddle, padded back-plates and a platform for throwing a lance if it was to be of optimum potential. As for the logistics involved in feeding these powerful beasts that consumed a minimum of 25 pounds of feed per day, half of it in grain, it would take too long.

Henry decided that he could not delay. He had to try to reach Shrewsbury before the rebel armies did. He had to risk it with the small force at his disposal.

At Shrewsbury the first sign that something was amiss would probably have been the departure of the Earl of Worcester with his army without the Prince of Wales. The young Prince, this 'sword-and-buckler' Prince of Wales, if Shakespeare is to be believed, who enjoyed 'cheap to vulgar company', 'hot wenches in flame-coloured taffeta' and who was the despair of his father, would probably have been a frequent visitor to the local taverns and his fate would now have been eagerly discussed. This until the news, which would have followed pretty soon, that three armies were marching towards their town, would have urged the inhabitants to consider their own fate.

Would there have been wavering loyalties? Perhaps! The period was not one of the written word. Only the clergy wrote down comments. Monks chronicled a sequence of events. Poets wrote, but carefully wrapped their critical words into sweet language so as not to displease their mighty patrons.

Chroniclers of the period, or immediately after, seem to suggest that Henry IV had been popular despite having acquired the crown by irregular means. Henry, in the year 1399 with the help of Percy 'Hotspur' (yes the same Percy who was now hot-spurring his way towards Shrewsbury) had wrenched the crown from Richard II. Private grievances, a deprived inheritance, banishment, were said to have been the reasons. Richard II, imprisoned at Pontefract Castle, was starved to death, some said. Murdered in cold blood, others said.

The chroniclers suggested also that Richard's disappearance had been of little concern as he had not been liked for many different reasons. Richard had lost Flanders. Losers of battles are never popular. He had been a spendthrift and effeminate. Despite being a lover of literature (Richard had been Chaucer's patron and benefactor) he had understood nothing of the country's needs. Under Richard's rule there had occurred the Peasants' Revolt and the first great outbreak of the plague (he can't be blamed for that!). Taxes had been raised unlawfully. He had tried to control rebellions against these taxes by repressive measures. Only one man had dared to speak his mind openly, they said. The poet John Gower had appealed to Richard to listen to his people 'instead of initiating purges and imposing censorship'.

As for Shrewsbury's position in all this, certainly for the merchants the loss

An illuminated letter showing Richard II and his wife Anne of Bohemia, in which, some interpretations suggest, his wife is pleading with him to look kindly upon the misfortunes of Shrewsbury. On display at Shrewsbury Museum & Art Gallery's medieval section. (by kind permission of Shrewsbury Museum & Art Gallery)

of Flanders would have been a major blow. In addition, Richard had also executed their benefactor, the Earl of Arundel, whose family had for generations helped the town politically. Through the Arundels Shrewsbury had gained its first seat in Parliament. Richard had justified the execution by claiming Arundel had been arrested and subsequently executed because of the 'great number of extortions, oppressions and grievances' committed against King and country. Shrewsbury's leading men doubted this. Arundel's arrest and execution had come too soon after another of Richard's 'forced loans' schemes not to create suspicions on that score!

Richard's lavish and ostentatious display when he had held Parliament in Shrewsbury during the winter 1397-8 had not endeared him to the townspeople either. He had arrived in dazzling splendour. He had entertained local dignitaries with sumptuous feasts. He thought people 'loved him'. They did not. They despised him, even more so after his military guards, the Cheshire men, had plundered Shrewsbury burgesses of their armour and proved a rowdy lot.

What they seemed to have quite forgotten was that in the year 1392 when Shrewsbury had been severely damaged by fire and many of the timbered and thatched dwellings had been destroyed, Richard, after an appeal for help, had been very generous. He had responded in a writ of privy seal dispatched on September 1394: 'regarding the damage and loss of his beloved lieges the bailiffs, good men, and commonality of the said town, he grants to them for repairs, freedom from their fee-farm for three years and other exceptions'.

But such is life. Henry IV represented hope of a better future and therefore (many said) had the support of every honest Englishman. Wavering loyalties? Certainly among the town's ruling bodies this question would not have arisen. In any case the Town Corporation had sworn the Oath of Allegiance to Henry IV. This was its duty towards any ruling monarch. This oath clearly stated 'no enemy of the King may enter the town except over the bailiff's body'.

As for the other inhabitants - would not the Prince of Wales's vulnerability alone have fired their passionate desire to protect him? Without a doubt! But what would happen if Percy 'Hotspur' (Traitor!) arrived at the town gate before the King? What if Percy demanded entrance and the bailiff refused to let him in, as it was his duty to do? Would Percy attack Shrewsbury? Percy Hotspur was the most renowned warrior in the country. What if Percy succeeded in taking the town? Would they take the Prince of Wales hostage? Would they all become hostages?

What if the Welsh army arrived first? The Welsh soldiers were said to be a ruthless lot. Savage, reluctant to conform to the convention of warfare, they drank and pillaged. The Cheshire men, now part of Percy's rebel army, had proved no better. Had they not stolen all the Shrewsbury burgesses' armour during Richard's Parliament here a few years ago? Henry's soldiers were said to be no better, robbing houses and churches - but at least they were fighting on the King's side.

What if Henry arrived first and Percy and the other armies besieged the town? Would they use 'wild fire' to try to burn the town down? What about food supplies? July, hot, hot days, harvest time. Fields of tall ripe corn, barley, peas. The soldiers would trample everything, pitch their tents on it. The winter rations gone! The livestock! Would they kill the animals and roast them for their dinner? There would be a bad winter ahead.

And then there was this to consider. What if the rebellion was to succeed? From all accounts, the rebels' armies, if they succeeded in joining together, far outnumbered that of the King. Would there be retribution by the *new* King?

All the Shrewsbury people could do now was to hope and pray that the King arrived before any of the other armies. Meanwhile, they had to strengthen the town's defences - the town walls, the Castle. The masons and every hand available must work from daybreak to nightfall for the benefit of the town. The guards must be increased to maximum capacity. Every available instrument to defend the town - axes, hammers, bows and arrows - must be made ready.

Although clergy and merchants by virtue of their vocation in either church or business were exempt from military summons, when it came to defend their town every burgess, of whatever occupation, was obliged to carry arms. (One assumes the armour stolen by Richard's military guards during the Parliament of 1397/8 had meanwhile been replaced). Every burgess was expected to do his duty. Every burgess would!

But there were some burgesses who were not allowed to carry arms, who were not allowed to do guard duties - by order of the King.......

Part II – The Rebels

Shrewsbury, ever since the Middle Ages, had represented a magnet for English and Welsh people from the surrounding area in search of a better life. Many had settled and achieved burgess status. Yet since Henry IV's usurpation four years before, disharmony had been sown.

Various factors had contributed to this. Not everybody saw Henry's acquisition of the crown by force as a positive development. To many Welsh, Arundel indeed seemed an 'oppressive and fickle' landlord. Richard, many thought, had been on their side while Henry, they felt, was not. The execution of Arundel 'for extortions, oppressions and grievances' seemed to them entirely justified.

Arundel's execution had left a power vacuum in the border country. The charismatic Welsh squire, Owen Glyndwr, said to have been a direct descendant of the Princes of Powys, saw an opportunity. He had been a member of Arundel's military retinue, had accompanied him to Scotland and France and was therefore well versed in matters of war. Glyndwr tried his luck by claiming part of Arundel's territory. In addition he also put in a claim for the territory of Reginald de Grey of Ruthin. Best go about this while Henry's position was still weak, he probably argued to himself.

The dispute over territory between Glyndwr and Reginald de Grey was put before the King. Henry took his time. Too long for Glyndwr who felt this was more than just a case of Royal Administration being slow. He took matters into his own hands. He gathered some of his relations, retainers and friends, burnt down Reginald de Grey's Ruthin estate and claimed a ransom of £6000 for Reginald's release.

Henry had travelled with his army to Wales intending to defeat this 'upstart' Glyndwr in battle. He had failed. It was impossible to engage in battle with an army such as Glyndwr's that just disappeared into the barren mountains when you wanted to confront it.

Welsh and English border disputes were nothing unusual but this new leader, who some claimed had mystic powers (the prerogative of Kings alone), represented a real threat. Especially since he appeared to attract ordinary Welsh people and managed to stir sentiments within their hearts not conducive to an ordered Kingdom.

Henry had to find means of controlling this. It was for that reason that a Parliamentary decree was issued to all the border towns in September 1402:

> '*No Welshman entirely born in Wales, having father and mother born in Wales, is allowed to purchase lands or tenements in the towns of Chester, Shrewsbury, Bridgnorth, Ludlow or any of the market towns adjoining Wales. No Welshman is to be received as citizen or burgess in any of these 'burghs'. Welshmen already living in such a 'burgh' or being citizens or burgesses, have to find surety for good bearing towards lord, King and the realm of England. No Welshman is to be accepted to the office of 'maire, bailiff, chamberlain or warden of gates or gaol'. And no Welshman is allowed to bear armour in any of the 'burghs'.*

The outcome of the decree, however, was not as Henry would have wanted. Instead of the unruly sentiments abating, patriotism as never known before started to grow. It became rumoured that Welsh scholars were withdrawing from Oxford and Cambridge, that they were gathering Welsh labourers working in England and encouraging their return to Wales to support Glyndwr. Was Glyndwr building an army?

Glyndwr had in fact made his private quarrel with Grey into a public mission to free his people from the 'yoke of oppression'. A people, impoverished by the recent ravages of the plague, only too ready to follow. But as yet it was only Glyndwr against Henry. This was soon to change.

Glyndwr and his army had captured one of the most powerful Marcher Lords, Mortimer, and held him to ransom. Henry had refused to pay the ransom demanded for Mortimer. In truth, he had no choice. He had only just paid a £6000 ransom for Grey and the war with Scotland and France had left the Royal coffers almost empty.

As a consequence of Henry's refusal to pay, Mortimer changed loyalties. He married Glyndwr's daughter. Percy, stationed at Chester in charge of keeping the Welsh under control, was related to Mortimer by marriage. Percy (of the Northumberland dynasty) also had an axe to grind with the King. He had been refused profits from the ransom of Scottish prisoners. Thus Mortimer, Percy and his Northumbrian kinsmen invited Glyndwr to join as partner in a rebellion to usurp Henry.

The prospects for a successful bid for the crown looked favourable. The rebels believed they had justice on their side. Not only had the dethroned Richard elected Mortimer's nephew Edmund as his successor, if strict heredity rules were applied, Edmund would indeed have been the rightful heir.

The rebels apparently made plans about how to divide the loot after their success. Glyndwr, it is said, had been promised the ancient district of Wales. Privately, it is said, Glyndwr was hoping to fulfil his dream of uniting Shrewsbury to Wales and restore its lineage with the Powys Princes. The supposed wealth of the town was also said to have been an attraction and, according to some mischievous tongues, so was the quality of Shrewsbury ale. The brewing industry had just taken off here in a big way. Probably each rebel had his personal agenda.

Meanwhile, Shrewsbury found itself in the middle. It might have had its fair share of tension since Henry had issued the decree about the Welsh burgesses and 'citizens'. How had Shrewsbury's people reacted to these discriminatory laws? Some inhabitants might have quietly ignored the laws. Others might have taken advantage, or benefited, like some traders as some customers avoided a Welsh connection out of fear. A Welsh maid in one burgess household might have continued to be employed, while in another she was dismissed. Possibly at the beginning only those Welsh attempting to climb the burgess ladder had felt the effect, but now, with an immediate threat to the town, tensions would have risen dramatically. It would have been difficult to be singled out as 'the Welshman who is not allowed to carry arms, or who is not allowed to stand guard'.

Part III – The Battle

Tomorrow, cousin Percy, you and I
And my good lord of Worcester
Will set forth to meet at Shrewsbury...[3]

Henry, one chronicler wrote, with an army around 30,000 strong (certainly an exaggeration), entered Shrewsbury over the English Bridge just a few hours before Percy's army arrived in the vicinity.

To prevent an attack on Shrewsbury Castle, the King who by now would have joined up with his son the Prince of Wales, ordered the suburb of Castle Foregate to be set on fire to prevent the enemy armies coming within reach of the town. Women, children and old men would have hurriedly left their homes to take refuge within the town, bringing with them what they could carry, tools of their trade, household goods.... shooing pigs, chickens before them while their homestead was going up in flames.

Percy, the same chronicler said, had seen from the Royal banner waving on the Castle walls that the King was in possession of the town. He therefore called off the attack on Shrewsbury and retired to the 'Bull-field', a Common which stretched eastward from Upper Berwick. He was probably waiting for the arrival of the other rebel armies.

Nobody would have slept that night except babies and little children. Breathing in the smell of burning timber the inhabitants would have watched with sinking hearts as the fire consumed a part of their town; homes and workshops turned into a vast glow of embers. They would have been kept awake by the sound of clinking armour and of knives, swords and daggers being sharpened. Anxious, tired and with eyes reddened from the smoke and the dust whisked up by the war-horses riding over the summer hardened earth, they would have awaited the break of dawn.

The King, it was recorded, could see, in the early morning light, the plain below Shrewsbury Castle stretching northwards glittering with the spear points of the hostile army. No doubt the inhabitants could see it too. And as they watched the King with the main body of his army ride out towards Hadnall they may well have mumbled a prayer or two.

The King had ordered the Abbot of Shrewsbury to talk to the rebels and discuss their grievances in a last attempt to avoid a battle. A discussion between the two sides followed; there was a feeling that Percy's rebels were biding their time as the Welsh army was still nowhere to be seen. But there was no avoiding battle.

Percy had apparently been told by a soothsayer that he would die at Berwick. At the time, so it is reported, he had naturally thought of Berwick-on-Tweed, but when he heard about the Shropshire Berwick, he was said to have been somewhat disconcerted. But honour was at stake. July 21 of the year 1403 promised another hot day.

Drawing depicting the Battle of Shrewsbury. (by kind permission of Shropshire Archaeological and Historical Society)

The exact position of the site of the battle is uncertain. A contemporary chronicler writes that the battle 'took place in a field of peas almost ripe' about two miles north of Shrewsbury. Recently a team of archaeologists suggested that the medieval village of Albrighton Hussey might have found itself right in the centre of the action.

The battle began. Soon the neat formation of enemy troops was broken up as arrows started to swish through the air out of a sea of armorial banners, shields and coats-of-arms. The latest innovation of warfare – the longbow, two metres in length of elm and very stiff - was specifically meant to confuse the enemy. Fourteen arrows could be dispatched per minute. It could penetrate the enemy and pierce leather and plate armour from a distance of 120 metres.

Following the arrows came the lancers; after that hand fighting with billhooks, swords and daggers. The fighting was accompanied by shouts of 'St. George' by the English and 'Esperance Percy' by the rebels. The Prince of Wales fought fiercely. He was wounded by an arrow in the face (because of the heat he must have removed his visor) but had refused to withdraw from the battle.

Two knights from the Royal army, dressed to look like the King (a method to detract attention from the true King) were killed and the rebels thought victory was theirs. The cry 'Henry Percy King' began to be heard, which one historian suggested, was evidence that Percy was indeed making a bid for the crown for himself rather than to secure the crown for the rightful heir, young Edmund.

Whilst lifting his visor, Percy was hit in the face by an arrow and killed. Shouts turned to 'Henry Percy, slain' and the rebel army dispersed. Glyndwr is said to have arrived meanwhile at Shelton. He 'ascended the branch of an oak tree to gain intelligence' but had arrived too late to change the outcome of the battle. There was no sign of the Northumberland army at all.

Details of the battle as described by the various chroniclers do not tally. But all agreed that it had been a bloody event with a great number of casualties and that it lasted for several hours.

The number of casualties given varies from 1,600 by the conservative estimator to 16,000 by others. Wounded, bleeding soldiers lay strewn within a radius of three miles. The loss of the right hand was said to have been the most common injury followed by the loss of an eye or testicles. Those who survived but were injured were probably dying slowly. Many were said to have dragged themselves to the Blackfriars near St. Mary's Water Lane in Shrewsbury where they died and their bodies were buried. Otherwise the bodies were buried in great pits around the battlefield area. However, no mass grave was found during a recent excavation in the grounds of Battlefield Church.

Both Henry and the Earl of Worcester were said to have wept at the sight of Percy's dead body. But on the following Monday when the war trials took place in Shrewsbury, the King ordered 'that they should either have the body impaled on a spear set into a millstone, or set upright between two millstones' in Shrewsbury to stop rumours that Percy was still alive. A number of earls and barons were beheaded, watched by the Shrewsbury inhabitants.

It took Shrewsbury a while to recover. Glyndwr continued to terrorise the surrounding area, sheep rustling and destroying crops, burning villages and suburbs right up to Shrewsbury's town walls. This added to the injuries already suffered by the Shrewsbury inhabitants who had seen Castle Foregate burnt. In 1407 Shrewsbury Corporation appealed to Henry IV, lamenting the sorry state of Shrewsbury:

1) *That half the town was now lately burned by chance, with all the goods of the burgesses in that part*

2) *At the Parliament held at Shrewsbury under Richard II, all the armour and defence of the burgesses were taken – damage 300 marks or more*

3) *Whereas the town was chiefly increased by merchandise, ale and other victuals, the sheep of the said country are destroyed by the rebels of Wales and the victualers of the town are destroyed because they cannot have deliverance of their victuals.*

4) *Owen of Glendowr burnt eight villages in the suburbs right up to the gates.*

5) *At the Battle of Shrewsbury, the suburbs on one side were burned, in order to save the town but to its great damage and loss.*

6) *Because of the frequent Royal visits which orders the burgesses to 'ridden in the best array' into Wales to protect the King at their own cost, without fee or reward, to the great impoverishment of all the town.*

7) *The said burgesses charged to watch the town every night, that many men have avoided the duty and left*

8) *Great floods so great right up to the wall, a great tower has fallen, to the peril of town, cost to rebuild £200 in repairs.*

9) Notwithstanding all great losses, the burgesses and commons have paid since the last Parliament at Coventry (1404) 400 Marks in divers taxes.

May it please your most sovereign lord, to consider the causes and mischiefs aforesaid, in relief of the said burgesses and commoners to grant that they be discharged and quit of taxes. [4]

Unlike Richard II, Henry had no patience with this moaning. He did, however, generously offer a quarter of the confiscated Percy estates to the town. Perhaps with the memory of the battle still in his mind, and conscious of Shrewsbury's loyalty to him, he fulfilled his longstanding promise to contribute towards the founding of a chantry chapel with eight chaplains on the battlefield of Shrewsbury.

And there is still stands, about two miles north of Shrewsbury, just off the A49, near the village of Hadnall, amid meadows of buttercups, surrounded by hedges of wild roses.

The Prince of Wales was to become Henry V, and was later credited with giving England back its heroic self-belief at the Battle of Agincourt.

Battlefield Church, North of Shrewsbury, with details from the church exterior: statue of King Henry and two gargoyles. The church is unique in that it is the only battlefield church to be located on what is believed to be the original site of the battle.

Tudor House, on Wyle Cop, where the Earl of Richmond is said to have stayed before going on to win the Battle of Bosworth.

Chapter 5

Back to Basics

1500 - 1600

In August 1485 the young Earl of Richmond, with a motley army of
4,000 Frenchmen, some Welsh, Lancaster- and Yorkshiremen, arrived
outside the gates of Shrewsbury demanding entrance. The bailiff of
Shrewsbury, Thomas Mytton, despite knowing that to allow the Earl of
Richmond entrance would be a breach of the Oath of Allegiance to King
Richard III, opened the gates.

The bailiff could not have been ignorant of the fact that the young Earl's
army that had landed at Milford Haven, and tramped across the mountains of
Mid-Wales, was a rebel army. However, it seemed the temptation to further the
young Earl's cause was too great. Discussion behind closed doors between leading
burgesses and the bailiff had probably taken place before the gates were opened.
Someone trained in the laws of the land must have realised that the wording of
the Oath of Allegiance to the King left room for interpretation. The Oath stated
that no enemy of the King may enter the town except over the bailiff's body.
However, the Oath of Allegiance did not state *dead* body.

Thomas Mytton, therefore, lay himself down and let the young rebel step
over his body. The bailiff had probably no idea that his action would determine
the course of England's history.

Why did he let the young Earl of Richmond in? An explanation may not be
hard to find. It seemed that after Henry IV's usurpation a century earlier a curse
had been unleashed upon England. True, Henry IV's son, the young Prince of
Wales who had so charmed the people at Shrewsbury before the Battle of
Shrewsbury, had brought honour and glory. As Henry V he had, for the first
time, engendered that feeling of 'Proud to be British'. However, after his rather
inglorious death on a French battlefield, death not by an enemy shot or arrow

from a longbow, but dysentery, anarchy had consumed the land.

Continuing dynastic wars (later to become termed 'Wars of the Roses') had ravaged the country. Henry V's own son, still an infant when his glorious father had died, proved sickly, refused to hunt and shunned the horrors of war. This had left the great Houses of Lancaster and York to fight each other with a bloodlust unheard of before and after.

And, as if that had not been enough, along came King Richard III. No worse shame and dishonour was ever known, they said! An 'unnatural tyrant', who forever twiddled 'his nervous ringed hand, forever half drawing his dagger from its sheath, with teeth gnawing his lower lip'. Richard was said to have had murdered just about anybody with the slightest claim to the throne who had not yet fled abroad. This included the little Princes in the Tower. It was said of Richard and his henchmen, 'The Cat, the Rat, and Lovel our dog; ruleth all England under a hog'. The wild boar had been the emblem in Richard III's coat of arms.

No wonder then the bailiff of Shrewsbury opened the gates to the young man. The Earl of Richmond, on that occasion, stayed in Tudor House in Wyle Cop, at least tradition tells us so. Here he refreshed himself, 're-fuelled' his army and subsequently went on to win the Battle of Bosworth, where Richard was killed. Richard's final words, according to Shakespeare, had been 'A horse! A horse, my kingdom for a horse!' [5]

The Earl of Richmond was crowned Henry VII. He was to prepare the ground on which England could blossom. His marriage to the Yorkist Princess Elizabeth Beaufort united the two warring factions and brought an end to the bitter dynastic feuds. However, it was his son, Henry VIII, who was to begin to organise the country according to what was then perceived as 'modern state management' practice.

Henry VIII had observed the rising stars of France and Spain. He now began to assess the potential of his own inheritance. In the year 1522 he ordered Cardinal Wolsey to draw up an inventory of all England on which were to be listed every man aged between 16 and 60, able and 'unable', their weapons and armour, if any, and any property they possessed.

The survey revealed a sorry sight – a population in decline, many without work; failed businesses; neglected country estates; towns crumbling and an extensive population of beggars. Shrewsbury was no exception. It was experiencing a slump. It was difficult for trade to flourish in a period when armies and robber bands terrorised the countryside. The wars with France had not helped either, so the wool trade had collapsed. Pirates were attacking shipping. The Drapers had not yet a monopoly and everyone was fighting over a slice of a very meagre pie.

Shrewsbury's role as a frontier town, now that Wales and England were united, had ceased. As a consequence the Castle was left to fall into ruin and the walls crumbled. The Abbey had a leaking roof with 'water pouring into the choir'. Town houses were neglected for lack of money for repair. Chimneys collapsed and toppled into the streets, endangering life and limb.

Parliament under Henry VIII began to shake up this ailing nation. The priority was given to build up military potential. An ancient law was revived. It stated that 'every Englishman and every Irishman dwelling in England was to have a longbow of his own height'. It ordered that butts should be made at every township where the inhabitants could practise their shots on all feast days. Anyone missing the exercise was to pay a halfpenny fine.

An Act was passed with the aim of revitalising towns. It was ordered that 'the owners of the houses in towns like Nottingham, Shrewsbury, Ludlow, Gloucester' which were 'in great ruin and decay, especially in the principal streets', and which now were too 'perilous for people to go by' were to rebuild them within three years. If the owners did not do so, the houses would become the possession of the Town Corporation, or of the first owner who entered them.

A Social Order Act was passed. It ordered that begging and vagabondage were to be controlled. The Act stated that 'persons over the age of 14' if caught begging without a licence, were to be whipped and 'burned through the gristle of the right ear with a hot iron of the compass of one inch about, manifesting his or her roguish kind of life…unless a substantial householder would offer employment'.

It stated that idle vagabonds 'were to be tied naked to a cart and whipped until their bodies were bloody'. A licence for begging was only to be given to friars, shipwrecked mariners and the lame and blind. A state project was to be launched to get the 'lusty and strong limbed into continual labour'. The project was to be financed by the Local Authorities.

How far these Acts were implemented is unknown. Successive Tudor

Governments were prolific producers of new laws, acts, rules and regulations on every aspect of life. But their bark was worse than their bite. They lacked the infrastructure to put their laws into force.

It is known that the exercises prescribed for longbow practice were eagerly followed. Shrewsbury's male population seemed to have rather enjoyed them. Practice sessions were held in Kingsland. They were combined with a few pints of ale. The men also tended to broaden the scope of the exercise by competing against each other in long distance shooting, or practise their skills on rabbits and deer in 'Ercall Park' which, being unlawful, may have been even more exiting.

As for re-building the ailing houses or getting the beggars off the streets, there was no money spare and no employment. Even Henry VIII and his ministers began to realise that. One can take a worn out ship and change around the old furniture, but in the end, only a boost of capital allows the re-vamping of the ship to make it seaworthy again.

Many factors contributed to the Reformation and the break with Papal authority: the invention of the printing press; the translation of the Bible from Latin into the vernacular; the expansion of literacy; spiritual conviction; economic advantages; Henry VIII's desire to divorce his first wife and marry Anne Boleyn. Whatever the interpretation one may prefer, there is no doubt that the break with Papal authority in the year 1536 represented a significant boost in the Royal coffers. Henry, by making himself head of the Church, rid himself of his strongest competitor. His chances of revitalizing the nation improved greatly. The Reformation could be regarded as one of the great takeover ventures of the second millennium.

Shrewsbury Corporation, through the Reformation, also lost its long-standing competitor, the Abbey. And yet people, it seemed, were not jubilant. Shrewsbury Abbey was among the last in the country to fall victim to the new order of things. At first the Abbot pleaded sickness. Then it was hoped that the distance from London would protect the Abbey community. However, on a cold January day in the year 1540, four of the King's representatives, burly men with whom there was no meddling, arrived at the Abbey with armed soldiers.

The Abbot and the seventeen monks surrendered. They signed the dreaded document, watched by the Shrewsbury inhabitants from across the river. And then began the dismantling of the buildings which for centuries had welcomed

Haughmond Abbey, about two miles east of Shrewsbury, also suffered under Henry VIII's dissolution of the monasteries. (by kind permission of Shrewsbury Chronicle)

pilgrims to pray over the bones of St. Winifred.

All the monastic buildings were either destroyed or put up for sale. Only the western half of the Abbey, because it also served as a parish church, was spared. The burgesses, it is said, pleaded with Henry VIII to be allowed to keep the Abbey as a residence for kings, or to make it into a school. The King would have none of that. The Abbey was sold to a Shrewsbury tailor.

The Friary buildings in town were not spared either. Some were changed into almshouses. Others were sold. The Collegiate of St. Chad was sold to a wealthy local family, who converted it into private housing. St. Mary's Collegiate was shut down. The proceeds went into the Royal coffers.

It could have been worse, though. Monks and Abbot were at the mercy of ruthless men. In fact, the Abbot received a pension of £80 and returned to his home at Bridgnorth. All the monks received small pensions. Many of them were re-educated into the new religion which at that period had hardly changed at all. It was property and its proceeds the King's men were interested in.

After Henry VIII's death, when his son Edward VI, at the age of nine, became dominated by religious extremists, things got tougher. A Shrewsbury inhabitant lamented in 1547 how 'the pycture of our lady owt of St. Mary's and the pycture of Mary Mawdelen, and the pycture of St. Chadde's owt of St. Chadd's churche, were all three burnyd in the Market-place'. Altars and crosses disappeared from their parish churches. The burning of frankincense, praying to saints, or the placing of candles before images were forbidden. Holy days came to be perceived by the authorities as a cause of 'much sloth and idleness, the very nurse of thieves, vagabonds, and divers other unthriftyness'. The annual Corpus Christi Procession, a symbolic reaffirmation of social order, was abolished.

Edward VI only ruled for six years. Following his death, at the age of sixteen, Queen Mary re-introduced the old faith and religious practices. No wonder there was hesitation among the population. A kind of wait and see attitude. For to be sure, when Mary restored Catholicism, the torn-out altars, crosses and images miraculously reappeared. A smooth amalgamation of the two ways to reach God continued for some time as long as the authorities did not interfere. The clergy remained essentially the same as had served before the Reformation. In some places in England bloody persecutions took place. Shrewsbury seemed to have been spared these.

Soon the benefits of 'new' investment money, the extra work created by all these changes, transformation of churches, whitewashing over the holy pictures, removing 'offensive' figurines, were beginning to show. By the middle of the 16th century Shrewsbury had recovered from the economic slump.

Once again Welsh ponies laden with bales of cloth brought their wares in great numbers. The cloth market was thriving again as demand rose. River traffic was busier than ever as orders for timber from Wales to build new houses increased. Timber was brought on rafts or 'float woods' during 'float water' (high water). Frankwell's wool processing workshops were again in a position to employ people. Perhaps, many a 'lusty and strong limbed' one time vagabond could now be seen washing wool fells in the Severn.

Private institutions now looked after the needy. The hospital of St. Chadde was maintained by the Society of Mercers. Shrewsbury Grammar School (today's Shrewsbury School) was founded in 1552 with donations from the Royal revenues derived from the one time Collegiates of St. Mary and St. Chad. The school grew rapidly into the largest school in the country, and civic pride grew with it.

The town's profile began to change. Lawyers began to set up their practices as the tasks, once done by the clergy, such as overseeing wills, fell to them. Many lawyers became, it was said, 'rich as drapers'. Perhaps it is symbolic that quite a few built their new houses from the stones taken from the now defunct Abbey monastery. Shrewsbury now had also a publisher and a bookseller.

Shrewsbury became renowned for its annual Whitsuntide plays. Under the Cambridge educated Thomas Ashton, headmaster of the new Grammar School, the performances took place in the 'Dry Quarry', where today Shrewsbury's swimming pool is situated. Plenty of other entertainment was bringing merriment to everyday life in town: bull-baiting, cock fighting, Morris dancing, travelling theatricals, dancing bears and acrobats, tightrope walkers, gingerbread sellers and puppet plays. It was said that so many people were now visiting the town, with the horse fair and the cattle drovers from Wales as well, that the stone bridges had become worn out by the wheels of the wagons and the hoof treads of the animals.

After Queen Elizabeth I took over the crown, and the new Act of Uniformity of 1559 made the Protestant religion and church attendance compulsory, life gradually became more earnest. Imperceptibly, the power of Central Government started to dictate daily life. Work hours, previously left to Local Governments to

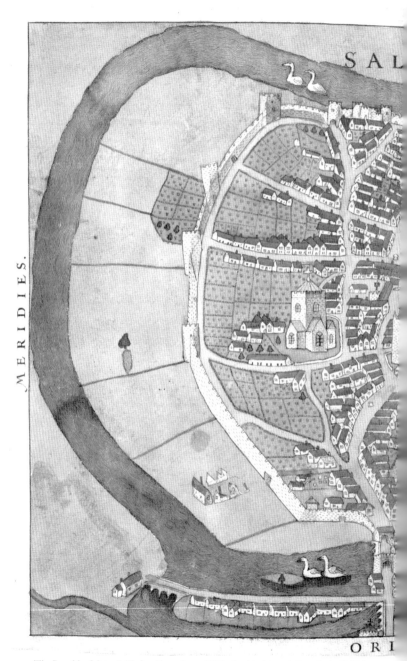

The Burghley Map of Tudor Shrewsbury 1574, (by kind permission of the British Museum)

decide, became nationally regulated. These were to be from 5am to 7 or 8pm during summer, and from dawn to sunset during winter. Every morning at four the bells of St. Mary's rang the people out of their beds, and every evening they rang in the curfew (original meaning cuevrefeu - cover fire), at 10pm in summer and 9pm in winter. Fire was still a constant hazard.

Religious extremists started to influence life in town more and more. The 'Puritans' as they were deridingly called, wanted to build a 'Godly City on the Hill'. The annual Whitsuntide play was abolished. Morris dancers, Christmas mummers and theatricals were looked upon with disdain. Alehouses, by then there were over sixty of them in Shrewsbury, were perceived as 'nests of criminality and idleness'.

Instead, the 'exercise' of preaching was introduced in St. Chad's in 1574. Everybody who wanted to be anybody had to be seen to attend. A John Tomkys, incumbent of St. Mary's, was said by some of the burgesses to be a particularly painful preacher of Protestant ethics.

A rebellion erupted over the customary annual Shearman tree celebration by the Shrewsbury cloth workers. The dispute ended up in court. The court decided in favour of retaining the old custom, from which one may conclude that high authority did not share in the enthusiasm for religious extremism.

Social divisions started to appear. Some of those who had lived through the period of 'Pope is on' or 'Pope is off' might have asked the question, 'if they got that one wrong, is it possible that they got the social hierarchy bit wrong?'. Resentment at 'snooty boarders' from the Grammar School was voiced. Resentment that 'chambers were being let to scholars at an exceeding rent' so that 'no poor man can have any house at a reasonable rent'. Resentment at bringing in 'foreigners'. A sit-in in the Grammar School by towns' women protested against the headmaster for employing teachers from 'abroad' in favour of local talents. For a while, the authorities heeded the complaints and employed local teachers.

Over the 16th century Shrewsbury's population had increased to 7,000. The period had brought wealth to many individuals, and had seen the Church of England take roots. However, traditional social cohesion had gone. At first it started to manifest itself only in small ripples but it was to grow into a tidal wave during the following few decades.

Tudor Shrewsbury is still very much alive today. Some of the timber-framed black and white, or black and cream, buildings may look a little tired. Some may have expanded or have gables askew, especially those built during the early Tudor period, however modern technology keeps them propped up. As for the later constructions, the Elizabethan Market Hall, Ireland Mansion and the Drapers Hall, still look proud and upright in the same way as their original proprietors might have perceived themselves to be.

The Elizabethan Market Hall in the Square with Owens Mansion in the distance.
(Photo: © Danny Beath)

The Gate House – Council House Court, where Charles I stayed in 1642 directing the Civil War.

Chapter 6

Charles I and all that...

1642 - 1649

Charles I entered Shrewsbury, accompanied by his nobles, and 200 foot soldiers supplied by the Shrewsbury militia, on September 20 1642. It was not as joyful an occasion as it might have been. The town had enjoyed a good run of luck for almost a century and now it had every reason to fear this might not continue. The Town Corporation knew the King, the second in the Stuart line, had not come for a social visit. He had come to direct the Civil War.

Some inhabitants may have looked back upon the period of Elizabeth I as 'the good old days'. They may have lamented that a period of law and order had truly gone now. Queen Elizabeth, 'the Virgin Queen', had reigned for forty-five years. During her rule England had defeated the Spanish Armada and become a great sea power.

The 17th century looked very different. The Reformation, in hindsight, had caused far more than the removal of holy crosses and monasteries. It had sown the seeds for a re-evaluation of Crown and State as well as of religion. On the European mainland civil war (the Thirty Years' War) had been raging throughout the early part of the century and was still going on. England, it seemed, had been spared. However, by the 1630's, heated exchanges were taking place within Parliament. And now war between 'Royalists' (Cavaliers) and 'Parliamentarians' (Roundheads) had been openly declared.

Who the culprit was that caused the Civil War, even today's historians can't agree on. Some argue it arose between moderate and extremist Protestants. Some argue it was due to increasing resentment by local gentry against centralization of power. Others say war was simply the result of a flash of hot temper, Royal money troubles and forced loans. Everybody agrees though, there was little enthusiasm for it. Most of the population was reluctant to take sides.

Shrewsbury had been no exception. True, when Charles I had raised his standard in Oxford, indicating the start of the war, Shrewsbury Assizes had, under the then High Sheriff Sir John Weld, sent a declaration of loyalty. Yet that was more in the hope that the town would then be left alone. Shrewsbury was a thriving market town. It intended to remain so. After all, it needed both its King and its Parliament. Why now should there be an open war between King and Parliament?

Within its walls there lived both Royalists and Parliamentarians. In order to keep the peace within Shrewsbury the Town Corporation had decreed that 'no person of either side or party should wear any colours'. Independence from outside interference had been the town's primary objective. Independence and neutrality! They had heard enough by word of mouth or private letters about the horrid events in Europe. They could do without that.

The Town Corporation had thought that the best protection against war was to be militarily strong. To ensure this, the town's defences, neglected over the last one hundred years, were being restored. The gates over the English and Welsh Bridges were strengthened and the upper and lower gates of St. Mary's Water Lane repaired. When the news from London became increasingly more threatening, they made available further funds to prop up the town wall, increase the watch to 'twelve in numbers during the night and six during the day'. Guards were armed with muskets and halberds and placed at all the gates.

After the Civil War had begun the guards were further increased. Notice was given to all those persons who had 'door or breaches' through the town wall to repair these immediately. Citizens 'of ability' were asked to arm themselves and to treat all strangers as suspect.

However, the very fact of Shrewsbury's now perfect defences made it very attractive to Charles. He recognized its advantages, not only its strong defensive position and river transport facility, but also its recruiting potential from the Welsh Marches. He had good reasons too to believe that at least the town's leading burgesses would not refuse his entry. Had he not a few years earlier made the 80-year-old Thomas Jones the first Mayor of Shrewsbury?

A message arrived two weeks after the declaration of war that the King desired to visit Shrewsbury. The Town Corporation could not very well refuse the King entrance. They had declared their loyalty to him. If now they refused they would be regarded as 'Parliamentarian' sympathizers, traitors and enemies, which would not bode well for the future. Shrewsbury Corporation's attitude therefore was that they just had to make the best of it. 'The town will make the best entertynment these troublesome times aforde', they said.

It was in the Gate House at Council House Court, the residence of the Lord President of the Council of the Marches, that the King took up lodgings. Further accommodation for the King's noblemen was found in the houses of schoolmasters and at the house of the Shrewsbury School headmaster. The Duke of York was lodged at the house of Master Jones the lawyer, who resided opposite St. Mary's Church.

The King wasted no time. He went out to greet his subjects. He went to address the crowd who had been gathering in Gay Meadow. The King was accompanied by his son the Prince of Wales, who was then just twelve years old. There he vied for the hearts, the heads and the financial support of the people. He promised them that he would melt down his own plates and sell his own lands to fight for his just rights and the just rights of his subjects. He invited everybody to do likewise. The revenue would be used to pay for the Royalist soldiers.

The country gentry, in particular, were invited to pay their respects. Records reveal that local landowners, against a donation of £6,000, gained a patent of peerage. A donation of a 'purse of gold' was rewarded with a knighthood.

And now the race began to make Shrewsbury a Royalist stronghold. All the gunsmiths were commanded to work in Shrewsbury or within its proximity. They were not allowed to make muskets or pistols for anyone but the King. Cartloads of arms were collected from North Wales and delivered to Shrewsbury to be stored. Soldiers were recruited from the surrounding region to build up an army of 6,000 foot soldiers and 2,000 horsemen.

Within a few days the town was transformed into a hive of frenzied activity. Apart from the noise, the sound of hammer blows, the hiss of red hot metal, the rattling of carts loaded with arms, the clang of coins being stamped in the Mint especially ordered from Aberystwyth, the town was grossly overcrowded.

This was not only due to the presence of the Royal Party and the extra workforce needed to produce arms, but also due to the nobility, knights and baronets from surrounding areas seeking protection within the walls of Shrewsbury.

Charles I stayed for two weeks only. But he kept a close watch on the town from afar. He ordered that one of the militia leaders should be sacked because he felt he was not committed to the cause. He ordered a further strengthening of Shrewsbury's defences and an increase in numbers of the town garrison.

This all put a heavy burden on the Town Corporation's shoulders. It had no choice but to increase taxes to pay for what was demanded. The inhabitants were beginning to feel frustrated.

No sooner had they come to terms with it, when Prince Rupert, a German nephew of Charles, arrived. He stayed at the Mayor's home, 'Jones Mansion'. Prince Rupert, young, energetic, with experience of active service in the Thirty Years' War in Europe, was a ruthless taskmaster. He imposed an even tighter grip on the inhabitants. He ordered that £1,000 must be raised for his troops. The burgesses were forced to sign a declaration and swear that they would withstand any rebellion against King Charles I. Anyone refusing to sign the declaration was threatened with death. It was said that a number of burgesses left the town.

Before Charles had departed Shrewsbury he had promised the Town Corporation that no inhabitants needed to billet soldiers in their homes. For this promise the Corporation had paid the King a lump sum of silver. Prince Rupert disregarded the promise. Soldiers had to be taken into homes. Frugal accommodation had to be handed over and homes shared with strangers.

For two years Prince Rupert moved in and out of Shrewsbury while in the surrounding countryside his soldiers were involved in skirmishes with Parliamentarian troops. Both sides terrorized the countryside so that trading virtually stopped. Transport from Montgomery, an area where most of the butter and cheese for Shrewsbury came from, was interrupted.

The crops in the surrounding areas were destroyed. Land could not be tilled. Rents could not be collected. Many people in the country lost their homes and livelihood. Many more sought refuge within Shrewsbury's walls.

By autumn 1644 Shrewsbury Corporation had had enough. Sir Francis Ottley, the town's Governor, sent a note of protest with a long list of grievances to the King. In it he protested at the breach of the promise that 'no free quarters should be putt upon them'. It stated that the town had no more money to pay for the production of gunpowder and the providing of coals and candles for the guards. It stated that the soldiers' horses had eaten all the grass in the meadows and

Sir Francis Ottley, Shrewsbury's Governor during the Civil War, with his wife Lucy and children Richard and Mary. (by kind permission of Shrewsbury Museum and Art Gallery)

pastures around the town. As a result the town had now no hay, most citizens had their horses stolen by soldiers and the town was in debt of over £1,000 because of the King's visit.

Shrewsbury fell to the Parliamentarians in February 1645. Not surprisingly, it had been an inside job. It is claimed that the Parliamentary soldiers had been led by well-known local men such as Mytton and Benbow.

A description of the attack by a 19th century historian mentions that town defences were scaled from various strategic points. One group of soldiers started to saw down the pales, surprising the guards who were said to have been worse for drink. Another group of soldiers, it is claimed, filed along the towpath by the riverside under the Council House, then made their way to the bottom of St. Mary's Water Lane where the gate, now aptly called Traitor's Gate, had been left open. They then advanced up the hill, past St. Mary's Church into the town centre, where in the Market Square, the main guard position was overpowered. The Governor, it is claimed, was surprised in his bed and taken prisoner. Within a few hours the Castle had surrendered.

That life under the Parliamentarians was no bed of roses either is another story. Charles I was executed on January 30, 1649. When in 1651 the then 21-year-old Prince of Wales (later to become Charles II under the Restoration) with Scottish help attempted to regain the Crown, Shrewsbury closed its gates on him. The town had had its fill of Royal warriors. The Prince of Wales was forced to continue until he reached Worcester. Shrewsbury avoided another 'Battle of Shrewsbury'. The battle was to be at Worcester.

It was from the Battle of Worcester that the young Prince of Wales had to flee for his life and it was during that flight to France that he hid in that famous oak tree at Boscobel. [6]

St. Mary's Water Lane leading up to Traitor's Gate, which had been left open to allow Parliamentary troops to overpower the Royalist army in town.

Chapter 7

The Plague
1650

In the summer of 1650 the plague once again broke out in Shrewsbury. The more frequent tolling of the funeral bell may have put the inhabitants on the alert. The possibility of an outbreak may have been but a rumour at first, whispered from neighbour to neighbour. Then the parish priests would have announced the dreaded news from their pulpits. The town crier would have carried it through the narrow streets.

It was three hundred years earlier, in the year 1349, that the first outbreak of the plague had occurred in England. During that time a third of the country's population had been wiped out. Subsequent epidemics had been less devastating.

That was of little consolation now. Images of the plague, hundreds dying, graveyards overflowing, the fear of being abandoned, outcast and the fear of death would have paralysed the inhabitants at first. Family members may have anxiously observed each other for the signs of the illness, fever, vomiting, the appearance of 'buboes' referred to as 'God's Tokens' because once they manifested themselves, God had surely marked you out to die. Neighbours may have watched the happenings next door, relieved when the smoke rose out the dwelling's chimney as usual.

Then questions would be asked. Why? How? Who was responsible for this outbreak? Nobody had as yet found an answer to these questions. Had not subsequent Town Corporations tried their hardest to prevent a further outbreak?

Health experts had long pointed the finger at bad air, 'Miasma', as a possible cause. It was for that reason that Shrewsbury's Town Corporation had already during the previous century ordered a new drive towards improved hygiene. All manner of action had been taken. The removal of all pigs and dogs. The slaughter of all cats.

It had introduced a more effective street cleaning programme. Main streets were to be cleaned every Wednesday and Saturday. Back lanes swept once a week. Dunghills were cleaned up and water ditches emptied regularly.

It had all been to no avail. The plague had re-occurred again and again. Someone, or something, must be bringing it to the town. Was it man, beast, clothes or goods?

And now, once again, strangers would be eyed with mistrust and avoided. The pedlar of household goods would be perceived as an enemy. Doors shut on him. Parliamentary soldiers, still stationed at the Castle, became obvious suspects. So would be the man of fashion who had just returned from London with a new periwig. Indeed the man himself would look upon his new periwig with suspicion. Could it have been made from the hair of a plague victim?

Everyone, everything, became suspect. The best way, and only way, to avoid the plague, it was believed, was the old and tested method. Leave the town. Half of Shrewsbury's population now packed a few belongings and left. But, unlike a couple of centuries before, when those left behind without leadership had rioted, the Town Corporation now stayed put. An action plan was ready. Procedures were implemented which were believed to be the most effective in containing a plague outbreak.

It had taken a long time to get so far. The question as to how to isolate the victims in order to stop the plague from spreading had always been paramount. Isolation of the sick as the first step towards managing the epidemic had, over the centuries, taken on various forms. At one time it had been thought that isolating people in their own home would be best. Infected homes were marked with bundles of straw. In later periods red crosses were painted on the doors. Subsequently it came to be perceived that keeping the sick in one place would be more effective. Thus, in another outbreak during the summer of 1537, at the instigation of the Council of the Marches, the sick of Shrewsbury were taken outside the town walls, where they were housed in a shed.

In a later outbreak this decision was reversed. Central Government's order was for infected houses to be shut up for four to six weeks with all members of the family, sick or healthy, still inside them. By the year 1600 this method was again reversed.

Increasingly Central Government had taken a hand in these matters. Its attitude over time had hardened, with strict laws and regulations increasingly put in place. The Plague Act of 1604 had given watchmen legal authority to use violence to keep people shut up. Shrewsbury Town Corporation now put these laws and regulations into action.

First a special committee was selected to monitor and oversee the progress of the epidemic. It was to meet at regular intervals. 'Searchers' were employed. These were to root out the afflicted. Searchers tended to be women. Ex-midwives, at one time called 'wise women', who, since the medical profession had been elevated and made an exclusively male preserve, were in need of employment and glad to be of service.

'Searchers' were to diagnose possible suspects, looking for the signs, the spots beneath the skin, orange turning blue then turning purple, the swelling of the lymph glands in the groin, armpits or neck, burning fever, bleeding from the lungs. It was not always easy, for the symptoms could easily be mistaken for other 'pernicious and contagious fevers' common during the period.

It was a life-threatening job, like that of a bomb explosive expert. But no applause awaited the 'searchers' for fulfilling their task. All those connected with plague victims would be shunned. Plague victims were outcasts long before death released them.

A few houses in town were designated as 'isolation houses'. The Cromwellian Government, after receiving the bad news, ordered that those people living in dwellings around the Castle should be evacuated and the nearby Grammar School closed. It ordered that the healthy soldiers stationed in the Castle were to be kept locked up inside the Castle compound while the ill, or likely to be infected soldiers, were to be moved outside the town walls. There they were to be placed into a field 'to lye till it be seen how the Lord will dispose of them'.

Guards would have escorted the people evacuated from the dwellings around the Castle to the 'Pesthouse'. The guards would of course have kept at a safe distance for fear of catching the disease. The 'Pesthouse', the special isolation hospital, was situated outside the town walls at Frankwell. Anyone with the plague buboes, or known to be from one of the 'isolation houses', found wandering outside in the company of others, was guilty of felony and could be hanged. The non-infected, if they dared walk in the streets, would keep in the middle, away from houses. The fact that grass was said to have grown in the streets suggests that few ventured out.

Critics of what often was perceived as inhumane treatment were severely reprimanded. And there were many critics. People by no means always accepted isolation without protest. One Thomas Browne, a Shrewsbury tailor, refused to be cooped up in an infected house. People in Frankwell in 1631, then the centre of the outbreak, rioted and tried to break down the gates and smash their way over the Welsh Bridge, but unsuccessfully.

An outbreak of the plague, apart from isolating the sick, created added problems. There was the question of provisions. Keeping up essential food supply to an affected town was not easy. Nobody wanted to go near a town that had the plague within its walls. This often resulted in food shortages. Volunteers had to be relied on. They would deposit the necessary supplies, such as wheat for bread, outside the town gates so that the inhabitants from this silent town where no wagons or carts dared to roll could sustain themselves.

Another urgent task of the Town Corporation was to announce the fact of the plague to the outside world. This had never been easy. The very rumour of the plague would bring a town's economic life to a virtual standstill. Fairs would be boycotted and, as a result, income from toll receipts diminished. The inhabitants from a plague-infected town would be refused entry into other towns and prevented from attending fairs there.

It is not surprising then that for many years Town Corporations had tried to cover up the existence of the plague whenever possible. It had become almost an unwritten code. During the 1576 outbreak, the bailiff of Bridgnorth had written a strongly worded letter to the bailiff of Shrewsbury demanding that he stop any inhabitants from his town from attending St. Luke's fair in Bridgnorth.

Trying to avoid a plague outbreak in the first place was paramount. To prevent possible agents of transmission reaching a 'clear' town, authorities resorted to all kinds of measures. During a plague outbreak in London, the Shrewsbury Town Corporation had issued a Proclamation that stated: 'Any person inhabiting within the town and franchise do ryde or go to the citie of London, or any place where the plague dothe remain, shall not return and come within four miles to this town'. The authorities had also ordered that no lodgings should be given to persons from plague-infected places and that no goods, flax, hemp, clothes, or household stuff were to be accepted from these places 'upon payne of disfranchisement'. In 1592 Shrewsbury had closed its wool market for a month to stop London merchants from coming into town. Wardens were appointed at every town gate to see that no unauthorised persons entered the town.

Central Government was well aware that many Town Corporations tried to cover up the fact of the plague. Thus in 1600 the Government made it a condition that financial help would be forthcoming only if local authorities agreed to a 'Cordon Sanitaire' during plague times.

During the 1650's epidemic Shrewsbury lost 250 people to the plague within six months. Most of the victims died in Frankwell isolation hospital. No evidence of rebellion or protest was recorded this time. It appears that by then the population had accepted its 'duty'.

This outbreak was to be the last. The plague had disappeared completely from England by the end of the 17th century. Whether this occurred as a result of the strict quarantine measures, improved hygiene, or whether there had occurred a biological change in the bacillus, or whether people had acquired greater immunity, these questions are still being pondered by today's medical historians.

The fact that the agent of transmission was the flea, carried by the black rat, also knows as the 'rattus rattus' ship rat, had not been recognised until much later. Indirectly, however, the measures adopted by the Authorities show that they were not that far off the mark.

The bacillus, responsible for the plague, 'Yersinia Pestis', was only discovered in 1894. At present British scientists are working on a vaccine against the plague that still occurs in South America, Africa and South Asia.

Chapter 8

A Veritable Jewel

1700 - 1800

The words used by Daniel Defoe to describe Shrewsbury in the year 1719 were: 'This is a rich town full of gentry and yet full of trade too. It is a town of mirth and gallantry'

Defoe's visit to Shrewsbury coincided with the publication of his first and most famous novel, *Robinson Crusoe*. A bestseller and just the kind of story to satisfy the appetite of a people living during a period when Britain was collecting colonies like trophies.

Some now call the period the Age of Reason and indeed it may well have appeared so after a century of confusion. Gone had the belief in the Divine Rights of Kings because God had not saved Charles I. Gone had the Military Government of Oliver Cromwell that had banned Christmas. Since 1688 a Constitutional monarchy had made the king 'the man of his people', not the other way round. The Georgian Kings might huff and puff, but Parliament would control them. 'Let them design military uniforms', some said. And they did. Crimson and gold braided, and tall, tall hats.

The Bible was now competing with travel literature. Travel, it was said, broadened the mind and Shrewsbury found itself among the most desirable destinations. It had, according to the taste of the time, all the ingredients to be considered 'picturesque'. The taste had been fashioned by the French landscape painters such as Claude Lorraine or Nicolas Poussin. The absolutely necessary ingredients were: a gurgling river where a few human figures dabble (probably Shrewsbury tanners' apprentices washing wool fells in the River Severn); sweeping meadows with trees amid which Pan could hide and play the flute; a dilapidated Castle on a rock and medieval church steeples surrounded by houses neat as pins.

Shrewsbury's geographical situation was compared to Italian hill towns, or to French fortress towns such as Avignon and Lyons. And while travel literature was eulogising the town's natural beauty medical men praised Shrewsbury's air as particularly health-giving. It was altogether 'a veritable jewel', according to one visitor.

Shrewsbury Corporation was not deaf to such praises. It did its utmost to oblige these valued visitors. To satisfy the taste for promenading it created 'Abbey Gardens'. It was soon to be praised for its gravel walks amid myrtle and holly trees, aloe, orange and lemon trees and its greenhouses filled with tropical plants.

The Town Corporation constructed the 'Quarry Walks'. Designed by the famous Thomas Wright, these elegant promenades along the river, shaded by lime trees so as not to compromise the fashionable pale skin of the ladies, became famous throughout the land. A 'Town Wall Walk' was devised. Kingsland was developed to allow the 'quality' to take an airing in their carriages while charming dandies accompanied them on horseback.

The walks in Shrewsbury were described by one visitor as 'the finest walks in England'. Kingsland was compared favourably with Hyde Park in London. The 'Town Wall Walk', one visitor wrote, offered panoramic views across the Shropshire countryside and the wild hills of Wales.

Defoe, fifty-nine years old at the time of his visit to Shrewsbury, after years of working as a secret agent, political pamphleteer, dealer in ship insurance, wool, oysters and linen and now finding himself for the first time financially secure, noted other advantages. Value for money. He wrote that he was impressed by the variety of goods on the local market. 'The greatest plenty of goods, provisions, and the cheapest in all the western part of England', he wrote.

It was not only visitors who recognized Shrewsbury's advantages. The local country gentry and nobility began to see benefits in owning a town house. They occupied them during the Social Season and during parliamentary elections. Most of the nobility had in one way or another benefited from colonial conquests so money was not a consideration. The Earls of Bradford had long had a residence in Dogpole. In 1730 the Earl of Bath, William Poulteney, had his splendid mansion built in town. These houses were built to reflect the grandeur of Ancient Rome and befitted the prevalent imperial state of mind.

It did not take long before the lifestyle of the wealthy newcomers and leisured people started to influence town life. Soon the rich locals joined in with enthusiasm. As a consequence a whole new range of services sprang up.

In education, young gentlemen had always had the 'Free' Grammar School to take care of them. At least in theory, for its reputation by that time had fallen to a low ebb. For gentlemen's daughters a new academy was established. The 'Chambre-Saxfield Academy' for gentlewomen was situated in Castle Ward, near St. Mary's Church. It took boarders and day pupils. The young ladies were taught music, sketching, and deportment, how to step gracefully into and out of a carriage, a most important skill considering the latest fashion, hooped skirts of several feet diameter and whalebone bodices.

A number of medical men, qualified in Paris (naturally) set up their practices in town. Among them a young man called Robert Darwin (Charles Darwin's father), who had studied in Edinburgh, Leyden and afterwards in Paris. His practice here as a doctor was to make him a rich man.

In addition, dancing masters, drawing masters, portrait painters (qualified in Paris, naturally) offered their services. A great demand for gardeners existed, not only to keep the public gardens perfect, but also to maintain the privately walled-in idylls of the gentry. Owing to personalities such as Capability Brown and Thomas Wright, gardening was becoming a respectable occupation.

Twenty-six barbers were said to have set up shop here by the 1730's to cater for gentlemen's needs. Despite the fashion dictating the wearing of wigs, the hair underneath had to be cropped short and the wigs cleaned. Perfumers selling pommades and liquid bloom of roses could be found in plenty.

Queen Anne had made the Social Season fashionable. Since then Shrewsbury too had taken up the baton. Horse racing started with the first racecourse at Kingsland. Later it was moved to Bicton Heath. Race meetings took place in September. The annual Shrewsbury Hunt took place in October. The town had its own pack of hounds. The annual Hunt Ball added to the social programme. Weekly evening Assemblies were first held at the Raven Inn in Castle Street, and later from 1770 onwards in the newly furnished, luxuriously decorated, gilt mirrored Assembly Room in the Lion Hotel where there were dancing, music and card games.

Tea-drinking parties became the latest novelty. Theatricals and concerts took place regularly. In addition to the walks, the rides, the games of bowls or tennis on the tennis court at Gullet Inn, an occasional 'Flower Show' took place, at which the most attractive carnation or the largest, most tasty, melon was awarded a prize.

The Quarry Park   (Photo: © Danny Beath)

And if there was still time, three bookseller offered their reading matters in town. The 'Free' Grammar School library had opened its doors to the public during the 1770's and was said to have had over 5000 books available. By November 1772 there was also the first newspaper, the *Shrewsbury Chronicle*, published weekly, as it still is today.

In maintaining the people of leisure and wealth, the non-leisured classes also benefited. Trade was booming for the goldsmiths and jewellers, fine cutlers, milliners, staymakers and tobacconists. So was that of the confectioners, or sweet shops, who offered Barbados clay sugar, brown and white sugar candy, sugar-pieces and double-refined sugar. The birdcage maker was also doing good business – it had become fashionable to own a green parrot.

Not only did barges now bring cheese and butter from Wales, but frigates navigated their way up the Severn from Bristol. At Mardol Quay these unloaded tea from India, tobacco from Virginia, rum and sugar from Jamaica, rice from Carolina, wines from France and oranges and lemons from Spain.

Demand for cloth was high with the extra amounts required to dress the King's regiments in new uniforms, and everybody who wanted to be somebody dressing their footmen in equally elaborate attire. The Welshmen with their ponies laden with bales of cloth arrived on Thursdays in larger numbers than ever. Welsh women wearing tall hats and red cloaks often accompanied them. The local textile workers were fully occupied.

The Town Corporation had plenty of money to spend on municipal services. The Welsh and the English bridges were rebuilt. New water supplies were installed. Oil lamps were erected in main streets. A new refuse collection scheme was introduced. Coal ashes, wood ashes, rubbish, dust, dirt and any other dung or filth which until then had been thrown out of the window into the streets, were now to be kept in the yard. Every Monday and Thursday the rubbish would be collected by the 'scavengers' armed with carts. They announced their presence with a hand-bell. The more entrepreneurial among the scavengers sold the muck on to farmers. Town muck was becoming popular and sought after since farmer George III had made 'intensive' farming a favourite pursuit.

Not everybody was happy with the new developments taking place in Shrewsbury. Especially by the second part of the 18th century some local people began to complain that the town was swamped with incoming leisured people

*Painting of a private garden in Dogpole, Shrewsbury during the 18th century
(by kind permission of Shrewsbury Museum & Art Gallery)*

whose feckless behaviour and spendthrift habits increased the prices. Indeed the 18th century 'leisured' class were renowned for acquiring huge fortunes abroad only to lose them in one night at the gambling table at home.

Most resentment by the law-abiding burgesses, however, was because they saw their political voice being denied. Honest local tradesmen, who for decades had given their life's blood to the benefit of the municipality, felt they were rejected as Freemen because, increasingly, the vacant places were going to those of wealth, especially local landowning magnates.

The 'Freedom of the Town' was considered a very important privilege. It was an honour and gave the right to vote during parliamentary elections. No doubt the gentry, who depended on these votes, carefully selected those individuals on whose support, political and financial, they could count. It was said that the Earl of Bath's reason for a residence in Shrewsbury had been politically motivated.

The period was renowned for what today would be labelled 'political corruption'. The Earl of Powys, one of the prominent people in town, it was whispered, wielded more power in the county than the King of France in Paris. During the 1759 Parliamentary elections there had been a lot of bad blood when the Earl of Powys and the Earl of Bath had been 'at each other's throat'.

Shrewsbury Borough records show that two rejected aspirants for the Freedom of the Town, a chandler and baker, had taken out a writ against the Town Corporation because their applications as Freemen had been rejected.

Over the second half of the 18th century Shrewsbury's population doubled from 7,000 to 14,000. As a consequence life in town became crowded. The once praised air had deteriorated because where earlier there had been empty spaces and gardens the poor had established tenements and crammed themselves in behind the impressive Georgian facades.

Many of the gentry began to leave Shrewsbury for other reasons. Roads and transport facilities had improved so rapidly that the attraction of London's social circles moved ever closer. More detrimental to the town economy was that the same roads that were taking away the gentry, were also taking away the Welsh cloth trade. London merchants now by-passed Shrewsbury and travelled directly to Dolgellau and Machynlleth to knock at farmhouses and mills. The middlemen of Shrewsbury were cut out. At first the Shrewsbury drapers were encouraged to fight back: 'Go out into Wales and recapture the market', they were advised. But it was no use.

Georgian Residences in Princess Street and Belmont. Note that some of the Georgian facades hide Elizabethan structures   (Photo: © Danny Beath)

In addition, competition from abroad brought the market into a recession. Whilst at first colonisation overseas had promised new markets and export opportunities, it soon was realized that cloth produced in these colonies presented a threat to the economy here. The first alarm bells had rung already at the beginning of the century when Indian calico and silk was brought to England. Ladies of fashion had adopted the exotic cloth with pleasure. In response to an appeal by drapers an Act of Parliament was passed to prohibit the use of these materials. For a while the danger to the cloth trade seemed to have been averted.

Then the War of American Independence interrupted exports. When America eventually declared independence that market was lost altogether. By the 1790's the spectacle of Welsh ponies laden with bales of cloth arriving at Shrewsbury became a thing of the past and the gentry had largely gone.

Many of the houses built in Shrewsbury during the 18th century are still standing proud. With hardly a bulge to give away their age, of red brick or wedding cake white exterior, symmetrical facades and sash windows, they have lost none of their charm. They can be found in Belmont, Quarry Place, College Hill and St. John's Hill among other places. They stand as testament to a period that for Shrewsbury was particularly splendid.

Chapter 9

Soul Searching & Philanthropy

1750 - 1820

Provocative thoughts had started to unnerve the tranquillity of the nation. Samuel Richardson, a London stationer and printer without the least knowledge of Latin and Greek, had published *Pamela*, a book about a servant maid. A servant maid! The immediate bestseller entered every nation's drawing room. 'Pamela' rage divided those who called it 'low' and dangerously 'levelling' and those who praised its humanity. 'Pamela' motifs appeared in shop windows on teacups, ladies' fans and handkerchiefs. They were bought in their thousands all over the country.

Much worse, the Rev. John Wesley was going about the country, travelling from town to town, preaching the irregular message that the poor should initiate their own salvation. He urged them to get their act together by becoming virtuous, by stopping drinking, swearing and fighting. He told them that their souls were equal to those of their betters and thus they too can be 'saved'.

A pleasing message indeed to be told one was worth being saved. A message, reviving like balm, to a voiceless multitude. To others - enraging. 'It was insulting', one lady of quality wrote at the time, 'to be told that you had a heart as sinful as the common wretches that crawl on the earth'.

Government and magistrates, too, felt uneasy. Words spoken out aloud to be heard by the poorest of the poor, most of whom could not even read, was even more dangerous than the 'Pamela Ragers'.

The Reverend John Wesley remained unabashed. He came to Shrewsbury for the first time in 1761. The house where he preached is overshadowed by the tall spires of St. Alkmund's church and St. Julian's. A plaque attached to the whitewashed terraced cottage in the narrow cobbled stone street called Fish Street states that 'The Rev. John Wesley preached here for the first time on March 16, 1761'.

Wesley House in Fish Street

This information, unless one is a Methodist, hardly sets one's heart aflutter and some may even ask, 'Who was this Wesley anyway?' Two hundred years ago most would have known who he was. He was that high profile preacher whose sermons about sin and punishment, hell fire and eternal damnation, salvation and eternal bliss caused crowds to weep, scream or faint with excitement; or, on other occasions, caused crowds to sneer, ridicule and riot. John Wesley was the founder of Methodism.

Now it has to be said, on his first visit to Shrewsbury the Oxford educated 'fanatic' with the glowing eyes, as he was described by some, found few fluttering hearts. His soul harvest was a rather meagre one. Although on his arrival at the little abode in Fish Street, believed to have been the home of a Shrewsbury currier (one who cures and dresses tanned leather) a large crowd had gathered, it was not the kind of crowd the Rev. Wesley would have liked to see. It heckled and sneered, ridiculed and laughed at him. He described it as a mob.

Wesley subsequently wrote in his diary that the mob's only purpose was to stare at him. He apparently managed to persuade a few of them to come into the house to hear him preach. Once inside, he wrote, 'they behaved decently enough'. He later concluded that 'preaching in Shrewsbury was like ploughing the sand.'

There may be a plausible explanation for this lack of enthusiasm. Wesley's message was primarily directed to the poor. To say there were no poor in Shrewsbury would be a great mistake. There were plenty of them - orphans, the sick, the disabled, widows, the old and those who managed to scrape a scanty living from the occasional labouring job.

But there was no mass poverty during the middle of that century when Wesley first preached in town. For most people employment was regular. The cloth industry was still doing well, so much so that the London Foundling Hospital had decided to set up a branch here. London orphaned babies and young children were sent here to be nursed and brought up until they could 'at a useful age' be apprenticed in the cloth industry'. Over 400 children were said to have 'found their way' to Shrewsbury's Foundling Hospital during the 1760's.

There was also plenty of work to be had in domestic service with the gentry and wealthy burgesses. No need to riot, as the poor did a few miles away in the newly-developing industrial areas around Wellington. There colliers, watermen and other labourers had many a time rampaged and broken into bakers' shops in protest at high bread prices before they were to have their own champion in the evangelist John Fletcher.

The truth was that Shrewsbury's poor were, in comparison to those in other areas, rather pampered. First, Shrewsbury had a great number of established parish churches to look after the needy, in some comfort, one might add. The poor accounts of Holy Cross and St. Giles suggest that on festive occasions the paupers were given legs of mutton and beef, wheat bread and beer. Pauper children, on their birthday, were given fourpenceworth of 'honey biskits and shugar'.

Equally important to the lives of the poor in Shrewsbury at the time was that the rich burgesses were very charity minded and the motto, 'noblesse oblige' was, it seemed, conscientiously applied. Already in 1724 Shrewsbury had a charity school. The Bowdler Charity School was founded by a rich draper of that name. It was to instill into poor children discipline and moral cleanliness, to look after their spiritual wellbeing and prepare them for their 'inevitable' station in life.

Millington's Hospital in Frankwell was endowed ten years later by James Millington, another rich draper. It served both as an orphanage and as a home for the elderly. It was a compact little community. The elderly were allotted two-roomed apartments, a patch of garden to tend, on which they could grow vegetables or just sit and watch the sky. They were also given 'a gown on St. Thomas's Day, a load of coals on All Saints' Day, and an allowance of £6'.

Millington's took in '20 poor boys and 20 poor girls'. They were clothed, fed and educated until the age of 14. After that they were found an apprenticeship and given a lump sum to help them start out. Millington's Hospital even offered a yearly scholarship for bright boys to study at Magdalene College, Cambridge.

The gentry and the 'quality' of the town, amid their pursuit of political ambitions and pleasures, card games and dancing, had found the money to build the Salop Infirmary during the 1750's. It was founded solely by subscriptions and donations collected before a Hunt Ball. After that, every year before the races started, the 'quality' would gather with the treasurer of the hospital at St. Chad's Church to celebrate its foundation. Further collections would then be made to keep it running. Medical men, of course, gave their services at the Infirmary free of charge, a custom that was to continue well into the 19th century.

With such an effective private social service system it was perhaps not

John Wesley preaching at the Market Cross
(by kind permission of John Rylands University Library of Manchester)

surprising that the poor of Shrewsbury showed a somewhat scant interest in the evangelist Wesley's message. Well-fed stomachs were less likely to ask questions. They did not feel neglected. They did not need the unconventional message since it seemed to them that established society looked after them well enough.

A small community of Methodists had existed in Shrewsbury since the 1740's. But, like Independents, Baptists, Unitarians, Presbyterians, Quakers and Catholics, they met discreetly. This was ever since the Jacobite Rebellion scare of 1715. At that time the Presbytarian meeting house behind some houses in the High Street had been attacked and a bonfire made in Frankwell of the timber from the house. Many non-conformists were excluded from official civic positions and universities.

However, John Wesley was not going to give up on Shrewsbury. He returned. His welcome was a little warmer than the first time. In 1770 he felt encouraged simply because no raw fists were directed at him. The Shrewsbury 'rabble' was less physical, they only used 'their tongues', he wrote in his diary.

When he came in 1781 following the invitation by the local Methodists to open their new preaching house, donated by a wealthy currier, a considerable crowd of onlookers welcomed him. One reason for this may have been that the *Shrewsbury Chronicle* had announced Wesley's visit in advance. Wesley noticed that the crowd was less hostile and was mildly pleased. But, he lamented, they did not take him seriously. In despair he wrote in his diary, 'All things are possible with God even the Christianising of Shrewsbury'.

A change of sentiment did gradually occur. This could have been as a result of the economic recession that by the 1780's had left many inhabitants uncertain as to their future. Economic recession was probably also the reason why the venture of the London Foundling Hospital had came to an end. In addition, with many of the gentry leaving the town to pursue their Social Season in London, business was less brisk. Above all, the doubling of the population within fifty years was stretching the resources available for the poor. Poor relief, once manageable enough, became a heavy burden.

Attitudes to dealing with poverty were changing. It became institutionalised. The empty Foundling Hospital was now converted into that dreaded workhouse, referred to as the 'House of Industry'. It was meant to encourage those who were admitted to continue their trade. But the poor of Shrewsbury very much

Portrait of James Millington, founder of Millington Hospital
(by kind permission of Mrs. Daphne Capps, Chair of the Trustees, The Millington Hospital Trust)

resented the workhouse. At first they refused to enter it at all. They would rather listen to the Reverend Wesley! The message of self-help was more appealing than the prospect of a place in the workhouse.

Certainly, on his last visit here in the year 1790 at the age of 86, Wesley found a large congregation had come to listen to him. Among them, he noted with satisfaction, were quite a number of 'quality' people. However, he never managed to 'Christianise' Shrewsbury during his lifetime.

By 1815 the Methodist congregation in the town was said to have grown to over 700 members. This suggests that his message had not fallen on completely barren ground. Methodism was to play an important role during the 19th century in many industrial towns. It encouraged the working people to help themselves and set up cooperatives to that end.

If the Government had been frightened at the Reverend's message because it contained the seeds of rebellion (although Wesley would have shuddered at the thought of it) far more dangerous thoughts were soon to come into the open. Shrewsbury was the seedbed where the next 'perpetrator' who was to rock established belief found his early inspiration. A little boy had been born on 12 February, 1809. From the moment he left his cradle he had refused all handed down knowledge. Dr. Butler's 'big school' saw little sign of intellectual brilliance in him. His father told him, 'You care for nothing but shooting, dogs and rat-catching and will be a disgrace to yourself and all your family'. The boy preferred to roam along the banks of the Severn observing beetles, spiders, fish and frogs. With the uncluttered mind of a child, he conducted his own experiments in the garden tool-shed. His name was Charles Darwin.

Of Shrewsbury's philanthropic institutions founded during the 18th century, Millington Hospital is still going strong as a private foundation fulfilling a function similar to that which it has been performing for over two hundred years. Health care and education have, of course, long become a State matter.

Charles Darwin's Birthplace on The Mount.

Wagons fording the Severn near Shrewsbury. Photograph taken during the 20th century. A way of travel common during earlier centuries.
(by kind permission of Shropshire Records and Research Library)

Chapter 10

Dandies in Ruffles &
Nankeen Breeches

1750 - 1830

Geography, so one famous French historian argues, is the determining factor of a town's fortunes. When on September 3, 1781, the newly appointed Lord Lieutenant of Ireland, Earl Temple, was given an official reception at the Lion Hotel, it certainly seemed that the town's geography had once again given it a winning hand.

Local entrepreneurs had read correctly the modern taste for, and need to, travel. The official reception given to the honourable gentleman had as much to do with his high office as with Shrewsbury's new achievement. For the Town Corporation as a whole, and the proprietor of the Lion Hotel Robert Lawrence, in particular, had reason to celebrate. They had captured a large chunk of the coach travel market between London and Dublin. The Earl Temple, for the first time, had chosen Shrewsbury as the official stop-over en route. This would surely encourage others to do likewise.

The Earl was said to have been 'extremely glad the Shrewsbury road had been recommended to him'. He had praised the accommodation in Shrewsbury as 'in every way perfect to his satisfaction'. This was sweet music to all concerned.

Coach travel had been slow in coming, not only to Shrewsbury, but nationwide. Although not new as a means for transportation, it was, during the early part of the 18th century, still perceived by many as rather effeminate. 'Does not a gentleman', so it was argued, 'sitting tall in the saddle, dressed in well-oiled jackboots, wrapped in a long coat, even if it is mud spluttered, look more manly?'

Also ladies often complained that travelling in a carriage, especially if fitted with glass windows, made them feel claustrophobic. Riding pillion behind a uniformed manservant, holding on to the belt around his waist, was, it seemed, much preferred. It was in just such a way that a party of three ladies, five gentlemen and six servants were said to have travelled from Shrewsbury to London in February, 1730. It took them twelve days.

Of course travelling by coach over roads which since the Middle Ages had seen little maintenance was a jolting affair. For while the Romans had the military to maintain roads and during the Middle Ages the Church had seen to the upkeep of them, Tudor and Stuart England had been rather neglectful on that score. Parishes, responsible for the upkeep of roads, did not regard them as a priority. The Civil War had given the already frail English road system a near death blow. Since then subsequent Governments had passed a long series of Acts and Bills. But only after the introduction of the new Turnpike Bill of 1745, so it seems, did things really start to roll again!

The new Turnpike Bill transferred the cost of road upkeep from the parishes to the road users. Everybody now using the roads had to pay, with the exception of the 'great guns' of the Army and Navy.

This did not go down well with some. The farmer who found himself having to pay 5d for 'calves, pigs, sheep and lamb the lot' when going to the market complained bitterly. There were the occasional fisticuffs when tempers flared at the gates. George II had been compelled to make 'pulling down a toll-gate' a punishable offence.

Shrewsbury's transport entrepreneurs, mainly local innkeepers, recognised the opportunities in the combination of victuals and travel. In 1750 a weekly wagon-service between Shrewsbury and Chester was established. The wagon, called a 'People Carrier', was fitted on either side with benches. It could carry twelve or more passengers. It was not the most charming way to travel but saved many a clog-heel.

Professional carriers of merchandise had long replaced their packhorses with wagons. The wagons were clumsy movers, heavy vehicles going at a snail's pace. Their wheels left deep narrow ruts in the roads. These filled up with rainwater that never seemed to dry out, to the annoyance of other travellers. If coach travel was to catch on, speed and comfort was of the essence.

The following decades saw the coach travel entrepreneurs vying with each other for the fastest, smoothest, best rides! Competition was great. The first regular weekly and direct public transport service from Shrewsbury to London started in April, 1753. It took four days and the cost of the journey, one way, was eighteen shillings.

The following year, Mr. Fowler, the innkeeper of the Raven, offered a stagecoach service to London with a journey time of only three and a half days. The price, however, at a guinea (21 shillings) was rather high. On the other hand, Fowler also offered cut-price travel on the same route for outside passengers at half price.

In 1764 a new coach model named 'The Machine' was introduced. It travelled to London three times a week. In summer the journey could be done in two days and a bit, with one overnight stop in Coventry. In the winter the journey took three days.

Five years later another model was introduced. The 'New Fly' was built on special steel springs for extra comfort. It offered a route via Birmingham. The coach left the Raven at eight in the morning and arrived in Birmingham at six in the evening. From there the overnight coach to London could be boarded. The cost of the journey was only twelve shillings. The actual journey time was just over 24 hours but it entailed overnight coach travel. Only the foolhardy would do that! Highway robbers were in their heyday!

In 1773 an even newer model, the 'New Machine', offered the fastest daytime route to London – two days with an overnight stay at Oxford. But at thirty-six shillings the journey price was rather high.

The London route was by far the most lucrative. Shrewsbury with its large gentry and professional population would have made good use of the services on offer. But it was the London - Shrewsbury - Dublin connection that brought most benefit to the town. Hence the celebration when the Lord Lieutenant of Ireland, Earl Temple, chose to use it and said he would continue to do so. It was like having received the Royal seal of approval.

Robert Lawrence, the Lion Hotel proprietor, justly took the glory for the route had been his brainchild. It was he who had sought out the landowners and convinced them that the project would spell success. It was he who had encouraged the upper servants in noble houses en route to set up inns along the road.

The route via Wrexham, Mold, St. Asaph and Conway was opened in July 1779. The service ran three times a week. The journey time from Shrewsbury was one and a half days and the fare £2.2.0d. Soon another, a slightly changed,

The Lion Hotel, Wyle Cop.

route was opened via Oswestry – Corwen – Llanrwst - Conway.

Later, when Ireland was united with Britain in 1801, Lawrence embarked on finding an even more efficient route, clearly foreseeing a necessary increase in official and administrative travel. The inhospitable terrain of North Wales, described until then as 'full of bad roads and bad inns' (many cottages still had no glass windows, only wicker windows), insurmountable natural obstacles and 'uncertain fords', with mountain sides falling steeply into deep valleys, was being surveyed. Lord Penrhyn, a local magnate, was persuaded to join the new scheme (some say it was the other way round). The new route, which took two years to build, went via Capel Curig. It opened in 1804. Lord Penrhyn, it was said, had 'a very handsome inn' built at Capel Curig for the convenience of the travellers.

Meanwhile Shrewsbury's inhabitants were getting used to the sight and sound of coaches arriving and departing from early morning to late at night, and to seeing tired horses panting up the steep hill of Wyle Cop. They grew accustomed to the sounds of coach wheels crunching over the uneven cobbles and the clicks of the coachmen's whips as they snapped, giving the signal to the horses to stop. They may have watched many a travel-weary stranger with curiosity and wonder, especially if these visitors wore the latest Paris fashions.

The arrival of the Royal Mail coach from London was the most exciting coach to watch. It was described as the 'King of the Road'. It did not just roll, it *flew*, over the roads. It announced its coming from a distance with the horn. The law stated specifically that the horn was to 'sound and blow as oft as the Post meets company or four times in every mile'.

The Royal Mail had an armed guard who carried two pistols, a sword and a blunderbuss. The guard sat at the back with his feet on the locked iron-clad mail box, protecting it with his life. A Shrewsbury traveller described one of these guards as 'one of the most swaggering fellows he had ever encountered, a true dandy dressed in ruffles and nankeen breeches and white stockings'. The writer nicknamed him the 'Prince of Wales'. [7]

To Shrewsbury, coach travel's economic benefits were highly welcome. The coaching industry provided new sources of income to innkeepers, shopkeepers and farriers, and employment to drivers, caterers and stable lads, all of whose business had suffered with the departing gentry. It also covered up the creeping underlying, economic depression that had bitten sharply into the town's prosperity since the loss of the Welsh wool trade.

It was not all plain sailing, though. Shrewsbury almost lost that all-important

Dublin route when in 1809, Sir Henry Parnell, a high Government official, on complaints from the Postmaster General, threatened to withdraw all mail coaches from using the Shrewsbury - Holyhead route owing to the dangerous state of the North Wales road.

During Parliamentary discussion it was decided to commission Thomas Telford to build a new road. Today it is the A5. A grant of £20,000 was provided. Only three years earlier Telford, the genius son of a Scottish shepherd, had finished building the magnificent Pontcysyllte Aqueduct near Chirk, part of the Llangollen canal scheme. He was now Britain's first professional road engineer.

Until Telford had come onto the scene, road building and road maintenance had been a haphazard affair. It consisted mainly of heaping gravel on more gravel where the mud had got the upper hand. But Telford paid attention to proper road levelling, drainage and to gradients suitable for coaches.

Telford had made it a condition that only professional surveyors and skilled men should work for him. It took ten years to complete the road to Holyhead. On its completion in the year 1819, one member of the House of Commons described it as 'the finest highway of the world'.

By 1822 Shrewsbury was heaving with coaches arriving and departing. Seven coaches a day left from the Lion Hotel for London alone. The journey time was now only 18 hours. In addition, there was a daily mail coach to Chester, Hereford, Welshpool and Newtown. There were coaches to Manchester, Worcester, Birmingham and Aberystwyth, which had become popular as a sea bathing resort (in 1850 the journey time was ten hours one way). There were also many private coaches, especially since the North Wales scenery itself was becoming a tourist attraction.

Each year the coaching fraternity celebrated their success on the day of the King's birthday. They paraded their carriages through the 'town bedecked with garlands and laurels' accompanied by musicians. They could not know that an engineer called Stephenson was experimenting with steam engines and that these were going to change their whole way of life.

The first railway, the Stockton-Darlington Railway, opened in 1825. It was soon to be followed by the Liverpool Manchester Railway in 1830 and the London-Birmingham Railway in 1839. Long before Shrewsbury had its own railway in 1848, which was to offer a five-hour journey to London, coaching traffic started to dwindle away, and with it, a revenue which was sorely missed.

A coach outside the Raven Hotel, Shrewsbury, during the late 19th century. (by kind permission of the Shrewsbury Chronicle)

Advertisement in Shrewsbury Chronicle, circa 1837 (by kind permission of the Shrewsbury Chronicle)

THE SALOPIAN COACH

EVERY Morning to BIRMINGHAM, at 9 o'clock precisely, from the TALBOT HOTEL, through Shiffnal and Wolverhampton.

Painting of Princess Victoria aged thirteen by Sir George Hayter. (by kind permission of The Royal Collection © 2003, Her Majesty Queen Elizabeth II)

Chapter 11

Princess Victoria

1832

It was just the kind of tonic needed. On 2nd August 1832, Shrewsbury had put on its most festive attire. It was expecting a Royal visitor, the thirteen-year-old Princess Victoria, future Queen of Great Britain. To celebrate the occasion the South Shropshire Cavalry Band in impeccable uniforms strutted up and down Wyle Cop playing 'National Airs' while a large crowd gathered at the side of the road. Everybody hoped to catch a glimpse of the Princess and her party.

She was a princess worth waiting for. Young and pretty, well, aren't all the young princesses pretty? It was more than that. She epitomized hope. Old men had occupied the throne for almost a century. Nobody would want to say a bad word against George III. His son, however, had not exactly inspired confidence, and after his only daughter Charlotte had died in childbirth it seemed they would never again have any luck. On young Princess Victoria therefore rested the hope that monarchial respectability could once again be established.

At the Shrewsbury Guildhall, meanwhile, the Viscount Clive and the Hon. Robert Henry Clive, the Mayor, members of the Town Corporation, Aldermen and councillors, dressed in their official robes of office, rehearsed their welcoming speeches. The Royal visit made a pleasant diversion from other pressing issues that for some time had occupied their minds. The main one was the vexing question as to what Shrewsbury's future role was going to be in this new industrial Britain.

For over half a century the Industrial Revolution had been gathering pace. Everywhere new inventions were improving the speed of production. In 1708 Abraham Darby had smelted the first iron on an industrial scale in a blast furnace at Coalbrookdale just a few miles from here. A steam railway locomotive had been built. The Coalbrookdale area had become the leading iron producing region in Britain. It produced iron rails, iron wheels, iron-bottomed boats and even an iron bridge. A porcelain factory had sprung up, a glass factory and a soap factory. [8]

In the north of England, Kay's flying shuttle, Hargreaves' Spinning-Jenny, Arkwright's water frame and Crompton's mule had all revolutionised the textile industry. And recently, everybody had started to talk cotton, cotton, cotton!

And Shrewsbury? Its staple resource had always been wool from Wales. Raw material for cotton cloth? Shrewsbury had no easy access to American raw cotton. It had no iron ore in the ground or coal. It had no steep gorges suitable to harvest waterpower. Geography certainly played a trick on the town this time!

Attempts at production had been made. In 1790 a factory for producing wool (cloth) at Longden Coleham was converted to weave cotton. It proved unprofitable. Linen manufacture looked more promising. A Leeds linen merchant, John Marshall, started a flax mill at Ditherington in 1793. Soon an impressive building was erected. The first iron-framed building ever. It had a tower which was then the tallest in the world. The first skyscraper! It was to be the first large-scale manufacturing unit in the town. It employed 500 people. [9]

In 1804 another flax mill was established in Castlefields and smaller flax mills, flannel spinning mills and linen mills started here and there. Domestic scale weaving, especially the weaving of corn sacks, also gave a reasonable income.

During the Napoleonic wars the extra demands due to the blockade assured full order books. Things were mildly successful. When, in June 1815, the Duke of Wellington won the glorious victory at Waterloo over that 'cocky little self-styled emperor' Napoleon, who was finally banned for good to the island of St. Helena, things, it was hoped, could only get better.

Shrewsbury, along with the whole nation, celebrated the end of the war. It had its own hero, Lord Hill, local Member of Parliament, who had been the Duke of Wellington's right-hand man at Waterloo. He had distinguished himself as the victor of Almaraz and on his return the town honoured the man with a permanent memorial - the Lord Hill Column.

Nobody could foresee that the end of the war would bring deep recession. Yet, the fact was that the sudden drop in demand saw prices of cloth and other merchandise plummeting like lead balloons. Only wheat prices were kept up artificially high by means of the 'Corn Laws' introduced by a Government made up primarily of landowners in whose interest the law was passed. These wretched 'Corn Laws' caused havoc to the poorer population and riots in many areas.

In Shrewsbury, the reality of the economic slump was not immediately obvious owing to its success as a coaching centre. Also a new road project, cutting right across the Abbey and gardens, was in progress under Thomas Telford. There was no reason to doubt the continuation of that area of income. The only heavy industrial concern in town, the Hazeldine foundry, was busy supplying iron for the huge Menai Bridge project. And there was beer brewing, an industry soon to be given a boost by the Government with the abolition of beer duty in 1830.

Shrewsbury thus did not experience a popular rebellion. No Peterloo Massacre occurred as it had in Manchester in 1819 when 80,000 protested against high bread prices and eleven were shot dead by the Yeomanry. And while travellers reported ragged children living in wretched huts among coal heaps in Wellington, just a few miles from here, Shrewsbury escaped the ravages of industrialisation.

Some unease, perhaps resentment at the new discipline required in factory production, may have unnerved the authorities, for the Town Corporation saw it necessary in 1820 to appoint a superintendent and twelve watchmen to protect property and keep public order. Perhaps it was anticipation of trouble rather than the reality of it that caused it to do this.

Shrewsbury Corporation was confident enough in the early 1820's to start improvements to the town centre. Oil lamps were replaced with gas lighting, flights of steps obstructing footpaths were removed, pavements were constructed and crooked street corners rounded. In addition, the stinking sewers, of which so many travellers passing through had complained, were at last covered up.

The twice weekly market was still a problem though. While in 1750 it had comfortably served a population of 5,000, it could not cope with double the size. Changes were made to improve the situation. The selling of horses was limited to Frankwell. The sheep market was moved to Castle Street, the pig market to the bottom of St. John's and Claremont Hill. The monthly cattle market, however, still created havoc in town.

The first really obvious signs of economic hardship felt in town were when the Corporation was forced to cut the salaries of its employees in 1828. Two years later the radical politician and journalist William Cobbett, anti-Corn Law activist travelling England on his political fact-finding and lecture tour, noted in his 'Rural Rides: 'It was fair-day when I arrived at Shrewsbury. Everything was on the decline. Cheese, which four years ago sold at sixty shillings, would not bring forty. I took particular pains to ascertain the fact with regard to the cheese, a great article here'. He also noted that the ironmongers were not selling a fourth part of what they used to sell five years previously and that the situation of the local weavers was desperate.

Cobbett had, of course, his own political agenda. He was surprised, however, at the interest Shrewsbury people showed in political issues. He wrote that he knew nobody in Shrewsbury and was not expecting much from his talk. For that reason he doubled the entrance fee to cover the cost of hiring the room. 'To my great surprise, I had a room full of gentlemen, at the request of some of whom I repeated the dose the next night'. 'Yes', he wrote, 'I was particularly pleased with the conduct of the young gentlemen at Shrewsbury'.

By the summer of 1832 the axe was hanging over the Castlefields flax mill with a potential loss of several hundred jobs. Coaching income was seriously threatened by the coming of the railways to the Midlands. The Royal visit was thus a welcome diversion, an excuse to put the pressing problems of the town's future on hold.

The bells of St. Mary's, St. Chad's and St. Julian's were ringing in unison as the Royal coach, drawn by beautiful grey horses, drew up in Wyle Cop. The page boys wore pink silk jackets and black hats. The horses' harnesses were pink silk decorated with artificial flowers. 'Hurrah, hurrah', the crowd shouted and all strained their necks to get a glimpse of the young Princess Victoria. She was accompanied by her mother, the Duchess of Kent, Baroness Lehzen her governess, and Conroy, the Duchess's private secretary.

At the Guildhall the Viscount Clive and the Hon. Robert Henry Clive, the Mayor and Aldermen made their well-rehearsed speeches. Then the Royal guests and their hosts moved to the Talbot Inn on account of 'the Court of Assize sitting in the Hall just then'. At the Talbot Inn [10] in Market Street the *Shrewsbury Chronicle* reported that the Mayor presented the Princess with a box of Shrewsbury Cakes. To the delight of the onlookers, the Princess opened the packet and tried one of them, offering one to her mother too. The town's chemist presented the Princess with lavender water. A Mr. Howell presented the Princess with a pair of crimson velvet dancing slippers.

While the Royal party lunched at Shrewsbury School at the invitation of the headmaster, Dr. Butler, who was famous for having turned the school from an ailing institution into a school renowned for academic excellence, the town officials prepared for the evening banquet. All the town's silver was taken out of store. The magnificent cup, which had at one time been given to the Corporation by the late Lord Clive, was filled with 'festive beverage'. The splendid silver tray, a gift to the town from the Earl of Powys, was filled with cakes.

The banqueting table was decked with the best 'hot-house' fruit of the season, amid other local fruit – strawberries, blackberries and cherries. The Earl of Liverpool had also sent a profusion of fruits from his own garden. The South Salopian Cavalry continued playing their 'Variety of National Airs', now outside the Talbot Inn.

The crowds lingered late into the night. The young Princess, from time to time, came to the window, smiled and bowed. The next morning the Royal party left for Welshpool and Powys Castle. 'The Princess had been plainly dressed', wrote the *Shrewsbury Chronicle* reporter, 'the people had been touched by the unaffected simplicity of the youthful Princess'.

The next day the members of the Town Corporation and the leading burgesses returned to the drawing board!

Princess Victoria was crowned Queen in 1837 at the age of 18. She was to rule for 64 years.

Shrewsbury Railway Station, one of the most magnificent buildings from the Victorian period. (Photograph: © Danny Beath)

Chapter 12

Floreat Salopia

1850 - 1900

When in November, 1859, Charles Darwin's Origin of Species was published in London, it did not appear to have caused an eyelid to flutter in Shrewsbury. All attention was directed towards finding volunteers for the Rifle Corps. 'Form, form! Riflemen form! Ready, be ready, to meet the storm…' read one of the calls for action in the Shrewsbury Chronicle. It seems, no sooner had the Crimea campaign ended, the French were sabre-rattling, and memories being long, Britain once again prepared to 'show France, or any other countries who would think of assailing us, that we are not just a nation of shopkeepers'.

In addition there was the inauguration of a statue of the great Clive of India. As to the Shropshire and North Wales Natural History and Antiquarian Society, it had just started to excavate the Roman town at Wroxeter. So who was Charles Darwin anyway? Who could remember the little boy who used to ramble along the riverside observing frogs and puppy dog's tails?

Some might have mocked: 'What do you expect from a place in the Shrubs?' For it was during this time that the interpretation of 'Scrobesbyrig' as 'a town in the shrubs' took hold. Certainly Shrewsbury's position in the national town league table had dropped considerably. Charles Dickens, the most famous literary figure of the times, considered Shrewsbury rather 'uncool'. In a letter written in 1858 during his stay here for one of his public readings, he wrote dismissively 'this place looks what Plorn would call 'ortily (awfully) dull'. The audience 'amused us mightily….the ladies were full dressed and the gentlemen to a man, in white gloves with flowers in their button holes'. Maybe Dickens, being a Londoner, felt a little restricted among the Tally Ho! set. Maybe he thought ideas did not flicker as readily into flames here as in London. But if he had stayed in Shrewsbury a while longer he might have found that here too human souls thirsted for knowledge of life and that here some Little Dorrit's warm heart was tap, tapping with the anticipation of bringing kindness into despair.

Shrewsbury was in reality, right up to the middle of the 1860's, rather rough with widespread poverty. Few inhabitants possessed white gloves. If they did, they would have found it difficult to keep them white.

Much of the rough influence was 'foreign influence', so some said. During the 1840's the Navvies (railway construction workers) had been in town. How could one miss them.....moleskin trousers, velveteen tail coats, felt hats turned up cheekily, red kerchiefs around the necks like butterflies. They had plenty of money to spend on drink. This was 'danger money', for their work was perilous, cutting tunnels, handling gunpowder, building bridges and cutting embankments. The Navvies drank like lords.

The Navvies brought women in their trail, older women to do the cooking for them, younger women for other reasons. As if the town did not have plenty of such women already. There was Roushill, referred to by many inhabitants as 'a vile den of infamy'. Half a dozen or more brothels were said to have existed there. There was Mardol, close to the Severn harbour where barge traffic moored. It was considered to be another Red Light district. Butcher Row was simply referred to as 'The Row' with a nudge and a wink. Over sixty prostitutes were said to have 'worked' the town by the 1850's.

As for the passages leading off the main streets, who could tell what dark deeds were going on there? In the old Market Square one apprentice butcher had killed another apprentice butcher in a crime of passion. At the Raven Hotel William Palmer had done his dirty deed. He had poisoned one of the guests during the Shrewsbury races.

Robberies were frequent around the new Railway Station. Assaults on police constables were commonplace (Shrewsbury Borough Police Force came into being in 1835). Vandalism, particularly throwing stones at railway carriages, had become a favourite pastime for bored youths. Thieving potatoes, coal or clothes was widespread.

As for drunkenness, it was not just an imported vice, whatever some wanted to believe. Perhaps the introduction of the Beerhouse Act in 1830 had something to do with it. It removed the beer tax. The Government's thinking behind it had been, 'let them grow hops and barley' to save the ailing agriculture. Alas, it did not prove such a good idea. It may have taken the recession out of agriculture, but the new beer shops' offerings sucked the energy and will to work out of many labourers. Over 50,000 new beer shops were said to have opened in England and Wales as a consequence of the Act. Eleven beer shops existed in the old heart of Shrewsbury, St. Alkmund's Square, alone.

In the dark lanes leading from it, the most prominent among them being Butcher Row, drunken men and women were said to wallow in filth and degradation. Poverty, many argued, was the result of this widespread drunkenness. The economic slump had not helped, of course, but something needed to be done!

It had taken a concerted effort, both by private individuals and the Corporation, to wrench the town into modern times. Vice, drunkenness, human suffering, had always existed throughout history, but the *modern* ethos was that they ought not to exist. The zest for reform, both moral as well as social, was therefore very strong in Victorian Britain. And certainly Charles Dickens could not have faulted Shrewsbury on that score.

One of Shrewsbury's leading reformers was Julia Wightman, the wife of the vicar of St. Alkmund's Church. She lived in the vicarage of St. Alkmund's and was confronted daily by the human misery caused, in her opinion, by drink and vice. 'Many a night', she recalled, 'we were woken out of our first sleep by the sound of drunken merriment and revelry, the shrill voices of the women among the crowd most conspicuous'.

Julia Whitman started to search Shrewsbury streets for young girls in danger of falling into an 'immoral lifestyle'. Often these girls were no more than twelve years old. Twelve was then the age of consent. If the girls could be persuaded, they would be taken off the streets and sent to 'Penitentiaries' for reform.

It was not an appealing lifestyle for the girls. Penitentiary life included solitary confinement, shaving of hair and a commitment to stay for two years. A jail sentence! Even Mrs. Wightman considered that regime too hard. Thus, in 1849, she instigated an alternative. With private subscription a house was bought on Wyle Cop. This, for the next eighteen years, was to become a home for vulnerable girls. Later the 'Institution', as it was referred to, was moved to St. Julian's Friars.

Julia Wightman also led a crusade against drunkenness. She herself gave up drink as an example. Beerhouses, she believed, were not the best places for working men to spend their leisure time. She started a campaign to raise money for a Working Men's Temperance Hall. She became a national figure of fame. She could count among her supporters the Bishop of Lichfield and Lord

Shaftesbury. The foundation stone for a Temperance Hall in the Market Square was laid in 1862 with great pomp and ceremony.

Individual efforts at improvements in town life were matched by the Town Council. Ever since medical science had pointed the finger at polluted drinking water as the cause of cholera (during the 1849 cholera epidemic Shrewsbury had lost 75 lives) efforts to prevent further outbreaks had been made. A special report was commissioned. It was published in 1854. Among its recommendations were faster rubbish removal and drain renewal. Gradually improvements were made.

The major problem of overcrowding, however, was not so easily solved. Property was in private hands. It was only when the Public Health Act of 1866 had given Local Authorities the power to compel landlords to install adequate drainage and proper water supplies that things started to move forward. There was a lot of haggling over the definition of 'nuisance' and 'overcrowding'. It was a question of changing values. The free Englishman's belief in the right to non-interference was difficult to overcome.

All improvements cost money. Revitalizing Shrewsbury's economic life was therefore perceived as paramount. But just in case the impression might be that Victorian Shrewsbury was too dull and too heavy in moral tone…a theatre had long existed. In 1840 the Music Hall opened to provide further entertainment, from literary readings and Handel's Messiah to 'the greatest combination of living curiosities: a giantess; a 'beautiful lady named Zoebida Luti'; comic songs, choruses, Banjo sketch artists, boomerang throwers and female American Negro singers.

The most important event contributing towards the revitalization of Shrewsbury, however, was the opening of the new Market Hall. It had been a long time coming. Strong differences of opinion as to the location of the market had delayed the project. Pride Hill, the preferred site, had been rejected by a strong lobby made up mainly of Frankwell and Mardol traders who had seen their income vastly reduced since the opening of the Welsh Railway in the early 1860's. The battle over the position of the new market went as far as London. The original Pride Hill plan was overturned by order of the Secretary of State himself!

Then there were accusations of extravagance against the Council! These

Victorian Market Hall, Shrewsbury, opened September 1869.
(by kind permission of the Shrewsbury Chronicle)

continued right up to the day of the opening. The Market Hall's final cost of £41,000 far outstripped the original estimate. But then it had all modern conveniences: an ice-house, a special cart-way and a ground-floor turning point for wagons. It was also planned to install a 'heating apparatus'.

The Town Council appeased the local residents whose main fear was that rates would rise. It pointed out that during the previous year the Council had managed to lower rates by twopence in the pound. Besides, they argued, with a population of almost 28,000 and an ever growing hinterland of consumers, they had every intention of making the new Market Hall a profitable venture to the benefit of all. However, as a goodwill gesture, the clock and bells for the tower, it said, were not to be paid for with council funds but through a charitable subscription, which they were glad to report, had almost reached its target.

Everybody was pleased with the end result. The Market Hall opened in September 1869. It stood as a symbol for new-found confidence after decades of economic stagnation. The town once again had redefined its role to the outside world. This new role was to be the leading market and service centre in the area. And Shrewsbury was intent on serving in style. The new Market Hall stretched from Mardol Head to Bellstone. In the process of its construction eighty dwellings had been knocked down. The impressive building was designed in the Italian style à la mode. The blue, red and white brick with a Grinshill stone dressing added a touch of glamour. The new Market Hall contained both the general market as well as the corn market. Gone forever were the unsightly 'booths, sheds and shambles' of old. The inscription in the town's coat of arms over the Mardol entrance read 'Floreat Salopia'.

The opening ceremony was going to be a splendid affair. All the town's schoolchildren were to take part in a 'monster procession'. There were to be sports in the Quarry followed by a balloon ascent and with fireworks display as the climax.

However, torrential rain lashed the streets in the morning of the official opening. In the afternoon a biting wind and heavy showers caused half the programme to be cancelled. Luckily, the weather could not spoil the official dinner.

Every dignitary of town and county had been invited. The menu, so the *Shrewsbury Chronicle* tells us, included mock turtle soup, giblet and oxtail, turbot

Statue of Charles Darwin outside Shrewsbury Library.

and lobster sauce, cod fish and oyster sauce, steamed eel, neck of venison, partridge and roast goose, trifle and Typsy cakes.

The Queen, the Prince and the Princess of Wales were 'toasted' and then all sang 'Rule Britannia'.

Today only Shrewsbury Railway Station is a reminder of the grandeur of spirit that motivated Victorian architects to design public buildings like Gothic cathedrals. The Victorian Market Hall, which would have equalled the splendid railway station, had become part of a lavish feast for the giant hungry jaws of the bulldozers of the 1960's.

In 1897 a statue of Charles Darwin commissioned by the Horticultural Society was placed outside the Shrewsbury Library, where it still stands. Darwin, in 2003, had been voted by a national poll among the ten greatest Britons ever.

Chapter 13

Town of Flowers
1939 - 1990

Members of the Shrewsbury Borough Council met in the autumn of 1944 to discuss the post-war future of the town. Local servicemen, stationed abroad, read the reports about the autumn meetings in the *Shrewsbury Chronicle*. Thus many were able to add their voices to the debate.

Lieutenant Bombardier Tanswell, stationed at the Burma front, wrote to the *Shrewsbury Chronicle* suggesting that priority should be given to clearing up Mardol and that a new traffic scheme should be introduced. Most importantly of all he wrote: 'I am all for making Shrewsbury a flower town. Let our magnificent annual Flower Show take the lead'. Spring flowers, summer flowers, evergreens, he suggested, should during every season decorate the town's square. An artillery man from another overseas battlefront wrote that his wish was that Shrewsbury should become renowned for its 'floral beauty'. He visualized window boxes, tubs of flowers and hanging baskets.

No doubt the council members took note and then filed the suggestions under 'pending'. For the moment more pressing issues had to be dealt with. A priority, one councillor pointed out, was the question of 'our girls in town'. 'Too many had been observed kissing and embracing airmen in dark lanes and doorways'.

There may have been a few coughs until another councillor raised the less embarrassing topic of the potential unemployment problem after the war.

'If there is one thing certain', he warned, 'Shrewsbury after the war will not be able to reproduce the conditions of 1939'. Did he mean the conditions before the war or the hectic demand on men and women's hands during the war? It was not clear.

It had been the season of village fetes, carnivals and the Miss Shropshire Competition when the news of the declaration of war on 3 September, 1939, had cut all the festivities short. Shrewsbury Carnival was cancelled. The cinemas closed. Within hours intercession services were held at St. Mary's Church. Immediately the Royal Salop Infirmary was put on a war footing accepting emergencies only.

Everybody was conscious that this war would be different from previous wars. That was the reason why for so long the Government had pursued an 'Appeasement' policy towards Hitler's German Government. The difference, anticipated by Chamberlain, was that whilst during the First World War, the Zeppelin raids alone had caused 1,400 civilian casualties, what would the damage and loss to civilian life be in an age of fighter planes, gas attacks and modern air bombardments?

The atrocities of war would come right into the living room. Indeed it was feared a war now would spell the end of civilization. Nobody wanted the war except Winston Churchill, who saw no alternative. Peace marches and peace rallies had been a regular feature throughout the 1930's. But now there was no choice.

Contingency plans to protect the population had long ago been drawn up but, as late as September, 1938, Prime Minister Chamberlain had felt confident enough to assure the nation: 'I believe it is peace for our time'. He had waved the signed document obtained at the Munich summit at a grateful public. He could not believe it would eventually prove useless.

And now the potential of aerial bombardment had to be faced. Shrewsbury was considered a low risk area but nothing could be guaranteed. Shelters were hastily being built. In the Quarry trenches were dug. Underneath the Market Hall a mechanical digger started excavating a bomb shelter as far away as possible from the clock tower, which it was feared could pose an additional hazard if it were hit.

The Market Hall shelter was expected to hold 650 people. Another bomb shelter was prepared in the lower ground floor of the Castle. It was to offer shelter to another 250 people. In addition, first aid posts were dotted around the town. Fireguard duties were assigned. White stripes were painted on pavement kerbs and a general blackout was ordered.

Then the official announcements started. The public was informed what it must do in case of air raids. 'Keep off the streets as much as possible; carry your gas mask with you always; make sure that you and every member of your household, especially children, have their name and address on them. If possible sew a label on their clothes so that they cannot pull it off'.

Shrewsbury householders were asked to provide a home for evacuees from high-risk areas. Most of the evacuees were to come from Liverpool. A weekly allowance of ten shillings and sixpence per child was offered. Within three days of the declaration of war, long, overfilled trains crawled into Shrewsbury railway station.

A motley crowd of evacuees, tired after a long journey in darkened trains, spilled out on to the platforms. Mostly these were schoolchildren. Each carried a rucksack, a gas mask and a ration bag with condensed milk and bully beef. The capable hands of the members of the local Women's Voluntary Service received them. The children were accompanied by their teachers, who had kept them quiet during the train journey with barley sugars. Mothers with children under five, expectant mothers and disabled people were also among the evacuees.

Shrewsbury, two weeks into the war, was described by one observer as a town in a 'military or semi-military garb' with streets 'thronging with soldiers, sailors, airmen and militiamen'. Schoolchildren from every social and ethnic background milled around the streets.

Shops were much busier than usual. Every day seemed like a market day with housewives buying extra food, searching for extra bedding to cope with the influx of strangers' children. In particular demand were 'Mackintosh sheets'. Only when dusk descended a 'Stygian gloom' was said to have enveloped the town. Motorists and pedestrians who had to venture out used the white ribbon on the pavement kerbs to find their way in the dark.

If there had been anxiety of war, increased activity had stilled it. During the following three months, more bomb shelters were erected. Brick was used as the town had run out of 'propping timber'. Bomb shelters could now be found under the Old Water Tower in Butcher Row, at Castle Foregate, at Shuker's in Pride Hill and Jay's in Mardol as well as at the Market Hall and the Castle.

Problems, however, surfaced. How to deal with homesick evacuees who grumbled about the strange taste of water in Shrewsbury, or the absence of fish and chips shops. Salopians had to get used to unaccustomed accents and peculiar city habits. There were the runaways who stole bicycles to make their way home, or the raiding of chicken runs by these 'Liverpool boys'.

Yet the year 1939 ended and nothing extraordinary had happened. The period is often referred to as the 'Phoney War'. It seemed almost as if there was no war on. Cinemas and theatres soon opened their doors again. Many of the evacuees had drifted back to their cities, often with little regret on either side. Some local people started to ask what all the fuss was about. Why should one be compelled to do War Duty when nothing was happening? Local militia leaders complained that a minority of Shrewsbury people placed sport and pleasure before duty.

In May, 1940, Norway, Denmark and Belgium fell to the enemy like a house of cards. In 'Operation Dynamo' hundreds of privately-owned little boats sailed across the Channel to help save the defeated and stranded British servicemen on Dunkirk Beach. Some of these servicemen were brought into Shrewsbury to recuperate. 'They were in an extreme state of exhaustion as a result of continuous marching and fighting for three weeks under an inferno of bombing', reported a *Shrewsbury Chronicle* journalist. They needed good food and rest to recover their fighting spirit.

France surrendered on June 18, 1940. These were dark days for Britain. It stood alone. Yet Winston Churchill, who had replaced Chamberlain as Prime Minister, was to call it 'Our Finest Hour'. It brought out the nation's determination to overcome and win. In Shrewsbury, a radio call for volunteers to form the Home Guard brought in more than 300 local men. It was feared that Hitler's forces might invade Britain. The Shropshire Maltings at Ditherington became barracks and training grounds as Copthorne barracks were unable to cope. A military hospital was also opened at Copthorne.

Most food supplies from abroad were interrupted. So was access to raw materials. In January, 1940, rationing was introduced. Everything was rationed except potatoes, alcohol and tobacco.

The 'Dig for Victory' campaign started. In Shrewsbury a demonstration plot was dug up in the Quarry. It was officially opened by the Mayor on January 1, 1941. It was meant to teach local householders how to change flowerbeds and lawns into vegetable gardens. Part of the Quarry was divided into allotments. Another part was used by the Corporation to provide vegetables for the 'British Restaurant' which offered school-meal like nourishment at a very low cost to all who wanted it.

Digging for victory. The Quarry Park became a field of vegetables during World War II.
(by kind permission of Gordon Riley from 'The World's Wonder Show')

Crowds at Shrewsbury Flower Show during the early 20th century
(by kind permission of Gordon Riley from 'The World's Wonder Show')

Soon the whole area between the main entrance of the Quarry Park and Porthill Bridge bloomed with potato plants and cabbages. A Domestic Rabbit Keepers' Association was founded to make tame rabbit an additional food supply (it having gone somewhat out of fashion since the Norman invasion).

The shortage of raw material was partly overcome by removing iron fencing all over Britain where possible. Shrewsbury Borough Council approved the taking down of iron railings around the Castle, the Guildhall, around St. Alkmund's Church and the Royal Salop Infirmary. The fences were broken up and sold for the manufacture of ammunition. (Had not Charles I begged the population to do the same three hundred years earlier?)

When the Battle of Britain raged over London in the summer of 1940, Londoners started to travel north, some seeking refuge in Shrewsbury. During and after the bombings in Birmingham and Coventry, Midlanders too arrived. In order to cope with this new influx the town provided further reception centres. One was opened at St. Alkmund's schoolroom, another at the Swan Hill Congregational Church.

Shrewsbury was hit by bombs twice. The first time it caused little damage. The second time, on August 31, 1940, a bomb destroyed a cottage on Ellesmere Road. It killed the mother and her two children. The father was pulled out of the rubble alive.

It seemed that not everybody was playing fair! Some found it difficult to accept the taste of second class meat. Or say goodbye to the lovely asters and sweet peas bordering their velvet lawns. Or refuse a prime morsel to 'Rufus' the terrier! The *Shrewsbury Chronicle* therefore published a checklist of patriotism. It asked among a long list of subjects: 'Have you made things difficult for your grocer or butcher by ....refusing to take your fair share of streaky bacon? Have you made any preparations in case all your windows are blown out on a wet night by an explosion? Do you give your dog anything which could be used as human food? Have you dug up parts of your garden to grow vegetables?'

When on 8 November 1942 the Battle of El Alamein was won and Tobruk recaptured, church bells all over Britain burst into song. In Shrewsbury, in addition, a procession by the Armed Forces, the Home Guard and Civil Defence Services took place.

Shrewsbury became livelier than ever. There was plenty of work, everybody was needed – women in ammunition factories, as 'Land Girls', as bus drivers. Girls and women had never known so much freedom and independence. There was plenty of amusement to be had. The Granada, Empire, Kings and County cinemas and theatres opened even on Sundays with films such as *Casablanca* with Humphrey Bogart, Ginger Rogers in *Roxie Hart*, Charlie Chaplin in *The Great Dictator*. Barbirolli and the Hallé Orchestra were frequent visitors.

But most of all the American servicemen brought a new dimension to town entertainment. They may have encountered resentment from the local males, if there were any left, but the girls had a brilliant time. The Americans, in a typical grand gesture, took over the whole of the Raven Hotel, lock, stock ,and barrel! By April 1943 it was made into an American Red Cross Leave Club. It had sleeping accommodation for over 100 servicemen. The Club's motto was 'to give the boys a real good time'. And so it did. Cabarets, dances, whisky on rocks the size of icebergs.

When Shrewsbury Borough Council was meeting during that autumn of 1944, D-Day was already in the past. Shrewsbury, incidentally, had been one of the marshalling areas for military vehicles in preparation for that important occasion. It had, of course, all been hush hush! The Salop Infirmary had cared for some of the soldiers during that particular offensive. The injured were brought in and the medical staff propped them up again, while volunteers supplied them with cigarettes and writing paper. Then Paris was recaptured from the Nazi army and victory was in the bag so to speak.

That was why Shrewsbury Borough Council was able to make plans for a post-war period before the official end of war had been celebrated. The subject of the moral danger 'to our girls' was urgent. For, as one councillor pointed out, in six months it may be too late! 'They were falling victim to war hysteria', he pointed out, and it was asked 'Should there be a curfew for girls under eighteen?' The curfew question was decided in the negative. Then for the first time the subject of sex education was timidly raised amid mortifying embarrassment until the agenda moved on to jobs.

Hundreds of local men and women, it was feared, would find themselves unemployed after peace was declared. Various possibilities were put forward. Attracting light industry into town, especially from bombed cities such as Birmingham, was favoured. Making Shrewsbury a tourist town, playing on the

'Gateway to Wales' role. It had served well enough during the Middle Ages and the 18th century. Attract tourists interested in historic buildings and railway junctions. Promote the town as a centre for shopping. Make it a town of flowers? And, by the way, the lime trees in the Quarry needed replacing. Two hundred years before the guidebooks had made them famous. They had served 226 years.

On V-E Day, May 1945, dance music boomed from the old gramophone in Market Square. To the tunes of Glen Miller, people surged, arms linked, up and down Pride Hill. New lime trees were planted in the Quarry.

By the 1980's many of the proposals made during that Council meeting in autumn 1944 had become reality. Shrewsbury had attracted light industry. This was helped by the improvement of transport links to the Midland motorways. Perkins, producing Rolls Royce engines, counted among the largest employers here for many decades after the war.

The so called 'slums' between Mardol and Barker Street have disappeared. The Victorian Market Hall, so proudly celebrated a century earlier, was pulled down. 'Rat riddled', it was said to be. It was replaced with a modern construction in the 1960's. Few now describe the redbrick clock tower and shops as pleasant. Many of the old houses, shops and hotels in town suffered a similar fate until the local Civic Society intervened.

As a tourist attraction and a 'Gateway to Wales' Shrewsbury has been moderately successful. The railway signal box occasionally attracts a railway buff! Traffic measures have changed shopping experience. It is a pleasure to walk up Pride Hill without car bumpers snapping at one's heels. Pride Hill was pedestrianised during the late 1970's and the High Street and Shoplatch have been cobbled , then uncobbled, and then partially cobbled!

The limes in the Quarry Park are in their prime once more. The Shrewsbury Flower Show, originally started by the Shropshire Horticultural Society in 1875, is the annual highlight of town life. A two-day spectacle of blooms, giant vegetables, craft and honeybee displays, motorcycle stunts, military pageants, Welsh choirs, pomp and circumstance and a magnificent fireworks display which every year seems to challenge the sky with ever more patterns and bangs.

In 1986 Shrewsbury was the winner of the Britain in Bloom competition.

A Town of Flowers – Hanging Baskets at the Boat House Inn.
(Photograph: © Danny Beath)

Containers as big as bathtubs filled with flowers during spring, summer and autumn decorate every square, corner and pedestrian area. Hanging baskets decorate town centre shops, public houses and private homes. The wishes expressed by the artillery men from the Burma front in the year 1944 that Shrewsbury should become a Town of Flowers have become true.

Chapter 14

The World within the Town

The World within the Town has been the leading thread running through this biography of Shrewsbury. Why biography? Why not call it a history? A history is a record and study of past events. A biography, strictly interpreted, is an account of a person's life written by another. A town is not a person. And yet it is a living body. It is made up of people whose fortunes and misfortunes are linked in experience. It is the interpretation of this experience between this body – this community – and the outside world that formed the focus of this work.

When 'Scrobbesbyrig' as a town was first mentioned in Anglo-Saxon documents the relationship between monarchs and burgesses had been very much that of ruler and subjugated. King Aethelred's visit and feast during the Christmas season in the year 1006 had entailed labour obligations. During the later Middle Ages, when Shrewsbury achieved wealth and status, greater self-determination and freedom had been bargained from the monarchs.

Since then there have been good times and bad times. The Battle of Shrewsbury may have marked a victory for Henry IV but the Shrewsbury people were left to bury the dead. The bailiff's decision to open the doors to the rebel Earl of Richmond was a high-risk strategy. It paid off and led eventually to a newfound civic pride. The Reformation forced the closure of the Abbey and would have been in many ways a disturbing experience yet it also enriched individuals and changed the face of society forever. Despite attempts to stay neutral Shrewsbury was drawn into the Civil War, but the town once again recovered during the 'Golden Age' of the 18th century. The Industrial Revolution once more caused the Town Corporation to re-think Shrewsbury's role as a town. Throughout its life the town's response to outside factors determined the fate of its inhabitants as a body.

And here the introductory paragraph in Charles Dickens's *Tale of Two Cities* springs to mind:

'It was the best of times, it was the worst of times, it was the age of wisdom, it was the age of foolishness, it was the epoch of belief, it was the epoch of incredulity, it was the season of Light, it was the season of Darkness......'

This work is only the tale of one town and much has been left unsaid. Yet it is more than just about good times and bad times. Over a thousand years dependence has given way to independence. No King, no overlord now to bow one's head to. The monopoly of the Church has gone. Self-determination is the keyword. Ah, now, wait a minute! Did someone say self-determination? Here and there one can hear a gasp, a chuckle. Whitehall – London – Central Government!

Never have there been more regulations. Housing targets! Planning controls! Laws on graffiti, chewing gum. Target books. League tables. 'Top Councils to be freed from grip of Whitehall', read a recent newspaper headline! In order to get privileges out of Central Government a town has to play its cards right. In order to be exempt from Council Tax capping it has to conform. Is this all that different from what it used to be for our medieval forefathers?

Ah, it is the people ruling for the people now. Party politics rather than the arbitrary moods of monarchs. In reality nothing has ever been all black and all white. Monarchs, if they were wise, always heeded the voice of the people. Parties in power today have to do the same if they want to be re-elected.

There are aspects the Town Corporation, or today's Town Council, can decide on independently. These relate to the most important question, 'What is the town's role in the wider world to be?' A question, which again and again, each generation has to ask and always will have to ask anew. In order for a town to remain a 'living town' its role has to be adapted to requirements not just from within, but from without. It cannot just ask 'What do we want for ourselves?' but 'What can the town offer to the world so that the world wants to come here?' 'Do we want the world to come here?' some may ask. Yes. Interaction with the world is essential. It is essential for trade, and trade has always been the mainstay of a town's existence.

What then is unique about Shrewsbury which may persuade visitors and tourists, or even people seeking a new place of residence, to come to this town rather than another?

Geography is still one of Shrewsbury's major assets. Owing to the restriction of the Severn loop the old town has essentially remained intact. Although much has been destroyed that should not have been, enough remains of its essential compactness. The Quarry Park with its tree-lined walks and flower displays was during the 18th century, and still is today, a unique asset. A 'veritable jewel'.

Country Life listed villages and country towns considered to be the 'best places to live in'. Shrewsbury must surely count among these. It is more than a country town. It offers delightful shopping facilities. Two large, beautifully designed shopping centres - the Darwin and the Pride Hill Centres - cut into the underbelly of the town so as not to spoil the town's aesthetic integrity. Within the old town are cafés, cosy teashops and smart eating-places. Wyle Cop, in particular, has become a specialised shopping street with individual small shops offering exclusive furnishing specialists, antiques and designer boutiques. An added bonus to Shrewsbury shopping is Shopmobility which allows shopping at leisure, with pleasure, to the less mobile.

An ever growing range of leisure and pastime facilities are offered. Victoria Quay, where once the barges and even frigates from Bristol unloaded fresh pineapples, oranges, tea and cheese, has now a number of 'Bar' type restaurants of sophisticated décor. A quay has been built, which during the summer, offers river trips.

Over the last few years a number of new clubs have opened their doors and the young, in long queues, the girls in little flimsy dresses even in frost and rain, wait patiently for entrance. They used to call them discos, but this is today decidedly 'uncool'.

The Music Hall, where Charles Dickens once gave his public readings to an audience he had considered 'uncool', still offers a variety of entertainments from Beverley Davison's Hot Strings, Dance Theatres, Anne Widdecombe in Conversation with Iain Dale, a Rock Show called 'Roll Out the Barrel', the Blues Brothers, to a Charles Darwin Memorial Lecture. Classical concerts and opera venues are regularly organised by the Shropshire Music Trust at various locations ranging from St. Mary's Church to the Lion Hotel's Assembly Room. A new theatre with modern staging facilities is planned.

The Shrewsbury Museum & Art Gallery (Rowley's House) has an excellent Roman collection from the Wroxeter site, a section devoted to Natural History with reference to Charles Darwin. It also has an interesting section about life in medieval Shrewsbury. Major redevelopment is on the way to make room for new displays. A Military Museum is housed at the Castle.

The Real Art Gallery in Meadow Place has regular exhibits by renowned local artists with a pleasant coffee/eating place. The Gateway Centre, as well as offering Adult Education courses of every kind, has exhibits by local artists, occasional concerts, plays and public talks and a very attractive tea/coffee/eating room with a terrace overlooking the Severn.

Facilities then, which make Shrewsbury more than just a country town. But is it enough to tempt new visitors? Every year the Shrewsbury Flower Show takes place over two days in the middle of August attracting tens of thousands of visitors from all over the country. The West-Mid Agricultural Show, held annually in May or June, is also a key date in the town's calendar.

In July 2003, the 600-year anniversary of the Battle of Shrewsbury will be commemorated. Earlier in the year Shrewsbury's football team had beaten Everton in the 3rd Round FA Cup and brought Chelsea here to face Shrewsbury at the Gay Meadow for the 4th Round. Shrewsbury, unfortunately lost, but the BBC cameras, apart from showing the game, once again highlighted the rich heritage of the town in brick and mortar, or wattle a daub! And it is this heritage that should appeal to visitors.

Shrewsbury has no splendid palaces of dukes or kings. Its history is of a more intimate kind, about ordinary people going about their business over centuries, adjusting expectation according to the times in which they lived. To preserve this heritage is not easy and not without expense. What should one do with ancient buildings which have outlived their purpose?

Shrewsbury's medieval church spires still welcome visitors and gladden the hearts of returning exiles. Yet with dwindling congregations many have had to find alternative uses. St. Mary's Church is today classed as a 'redundant church'. Occasionally concerts are held, and recently a major exhibition of Anthony Gormley's 'Field for the British Isles' was staged there. St. Julian's Church, until a couple of years ago, had served as an Arts and Crafts Centre. The tower has long been a private dwelling.

Shrewsbury Castle, for many years a seat of Local Government, is now a Military Museum. Occasionally on its lawn theatre performances take place. Bishop's Mansion in Butcher Row, the first medieval shopping centre, still retains its original use. One of the oldest buildings in St. Alkmund's Square, renovated to high standard a few years ago, houses the Civic Society. Exhibitions of paintings are frequently held in one of the rooms. A coffee-shop next door still retains all the original Tudor features.

The Town Wall, so often subject to attacks, had almost totally disappeared during the late 18th century when, along with smart new Georgian residences, the original Salop Infirmary was constructed. A tower, maintained by the National Trust, and part of the South wall still exist. A part of the town wall has been preserved in the downstairs restaurant of McDonald's. A section has recently been rebuilt near the town's Shropshire Records and Research Centre.

Tudor House, where Henry VII is said to have stayed before he went on to win the battle at Bosworth, houses an antique shop. The Elizabethan Market Hall is being renovated and awaiting a decision as to its future with much controversy surrounding it. The 17th century Rowley's House, originally a rich wool merchant's mansion, has long served as a Museum and now also as an Art Gallery.

The Gate House and Council House Court, where Charles I stayed during the Civil War, are in private hands. Gay Meadow, where Charles vied for the hearts and minds of the people, is the town's football ground. The residence in which Prince Rupert stayed, is now part of the Prince Rupert Hotel.

Wesley House is a private dwelling. The flax mill at Ditherington, having long outlived its usefulness, is awaiting a decision as to its future role. The Lion Hotel, where Lord Temple, the first Lord Lieutenant of Ireland had his overnight stop, is still one of the leading hotels in town. Where once the dreaded workhouse stood at the top of Kingsland bank there now stands Shrewsbury School, founded originally in 1552 with donations from the Royal revenue derived from the Collegiates of St. Mary and St. Chad which were closed during the Reformation. The Salop Infirmary has been converted into shops and apartments. The adjacent Nursing Home, the Victorian Eye, Ear and Throat hospital and a brewery in Coleham have all been converted into luxury apartments.

Above then are just a few example of how heritage buildings and sites have been adapted to modern usage. It is perhaps interesting to ponder here that whilst all human endeavours are subject to change, the swans on the Severn still wear the same white feathers as the ones drawn in the Burghley Map of Tudor Shrewsbury of 1574!

Since this biography of Shrewsbury as a town started with a party it might as well end with a party. Queen Elizabeth II's Golden Jubilee marking fifty years of her reign was celebrated at the beginning of June 2002. Several parties at Buckingham Palace, a classical concert, a pop concert and a garden party, were televised and most of the nation did partake. People lucky enough to have won an entrance ticket through a national raffle received a Royal picnic hamper containing Coronation Chicken and Champagne. Perhaps it was the attraction of the top pop stars rather than monarchial sentiments that drew the crowds? Who cared! Who didn't delight in watching the young Princes' timid blushes at a blonde beauty's warbling notes or at Ozzy Osbourne's boldness!

Shrewsbury held its own celebrations. While official functions for invited guests were well attended it seemed, initially, that enthusiasm was slow to rise. The official parade through the town with pomp and circumstance attracted, according to a journalist, 'dozens' rather than 'hundreds' or even 'thousands' of people. Was it the fault of the weather, or World Cup football? Or anti-monarchial sentiments?

Street parties, compared with the Silver Jubilee, seemed slow in coming too. Some blamed the interference of bureaucracy. The need for insurance dictated by the Zeitgeist which does not allow for accidents. Some blamed the Royal family's moral lapses (not the Queen's, of course) as if previous Royalty had been paragons of virtue, and as if virtue had ever been the determinant of Royal status. 'Do we want, do we need the monarchy?' were questions often heard until the date of the celebrations started to close in and hearts began to warm at the prospect of a party.

The classical concert with fireworks in the Quarry Park was a great success. So were the barn dances, fashion shows, fun days, Jubilee balls and Jubilee garden parties held privately or publicly inside and outside Shrewsbury as Union Jacks were unfurled and sausage rolls heaped up to the music of the fifties!

A Tea Party was held in the Quarry Park with the Alice in Wonderland theme. It featured a giant throne of flowers and the longest banqueting table in the

Swans on the River Severn, 1574 and 2003

world, 1,500 feet long. It stretched from the top of the Quarry down to the Severn. It seated two thousand children who were to share out among themselves a Jubilee cake fifteen feet in diameter. Everything co-operated except the weather. It rained in sheets almost the whole day! But a great time was had by all. Perhaps it had ever been thus. Royal celebrations - a good excuse for a Party!

Celebrating Queen Elizabeth II's Jubilee in Shrewsbury (by kind permission of Shrewsbury Town Centre Management Partnership)

Map of Shrewsbury showing some of the significant sites relevant to this work.

(by kind permission of Shrewsbury Tourism Association)

1. St. Alkmund's Square – the Anglo-Saxon Market Place

2. Castle and Tower (original 'Scrob's Tower) later replaced by the Norman Earl of Montgomery

3. Tudor House, where according to tradition Henry VII stayed before going on to win the battle of Bosworth

4. The Tudor Market Hall

5. The Abbey destroyed during the Reformation

6. The Gate House, where Charles I stayed whilst directing the Civil War

7. Gay Meadow, where Charles vied for the hearts and minds of the people

8. St. Mary's Water Lane, up which the Parliamentary army entered the town

9. Traitor's Gate

10. Quarry Park: 'A veritable Jewel'

11. Charles Darwin's Birthplace

12. Shrewsbury Museum & Art Gallery

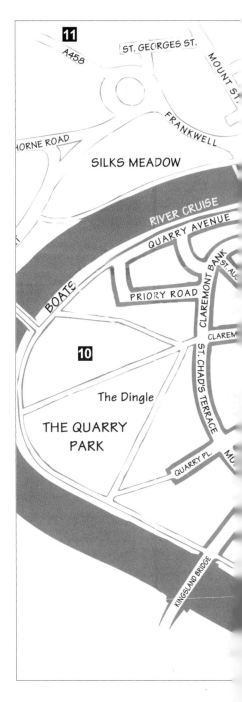

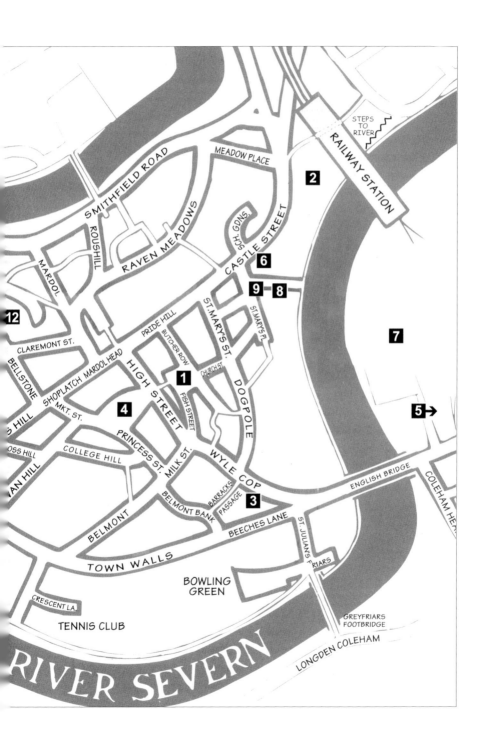

STEPS
TO
RIVER

RAILWAY STATION

MEADOW PLACE

SMITHFIELD ROAD

ROUSHILL

RAVEN MEADOWS

MARDOL

SCH. GDNS.

CASTLE STREET

2

6

9 **8**

ST. MARYS ST.

ST. MARYS PL.

12

CLAREMONT ST.

PRIDE HILL

BUTCHER ROW

7

BELLSTONE

SHOPLATCH

MARDOL HEAD

HIGH STREET

FISH STREET

CHURCH ST.

1

DOGPOLE

S HILL

MKT. ST.

4

5 →

OSS HILL

COLLEGE HILL

PRINCESS ST.

MILK ST.

WYLE COP

AN HILL

BELMONT

BELMONT BANK

BARRACKS PASSAGE

3

ENGLISH BRIDGE

COLEHAM HEA

BEECHES LANE

ST. JULIANS FRIARS

TOWN WALLS

BOWLING
GREEN

CRESCENT LA.

TENNIS CLUB

GREYFRIARS
FOOTBRIDGE

RIVER SEVERN

LONGDEN COLEHAM

Notes

1. Shrewsbury Museum & Art Gallery (Rowley's Mansion) contains all these artefacts and more.

2. Displayed at Shrewsbury Museum & Art Gallery, under Medieval Shrewsbury.

3. Henry IV, by William Shakespeare, Act 3, Scene 1. Shakespeare wrote a number of History Plays based loosely on actual events.

4. From 'A History of Shrewsbury, Vol. 1, Owen and Blakewell, 1825

5. Richard III by William Shakespeare, Act 5, Scene 6.

6. After Prince Charles lost at the Battle of Worcester, he escaped with some of his gentlemen through Worcester's northern gate on 3 September, 1731. The group headed north under the cover of darkness. One of the gentlemen recommended Boscobel (near Wolverhampton) as a safe haven knowing the people to be loyal and kind Catholics. However they considered the place too risky and the Prince eventually found shelter at Whiteladies Priory a few miles from Boscobel. There Charles was given bread and cheese and he changed from his buff coat and red sash into country clothing, 'a green jerkin, grey cloth breeches, leather doublet and greasy soft hat', to resemble a woodman. His only problem apparently had been the socks and shoes. The Prince was over six ft. tall. He kept his own socks but in order to disguise their Royal origin tore off the embroidery. All the shoes brought to him were too small so he had to tear off the toe part to allow him to walk. The Prince's discarded Royal clothes were flung into a privy-house in accordance to his orders! Now under the name of Will Jones, having separated from most of his companions for safety, Charles crisscrossed the countryside in an attempt to find an escape route to France. The preferred Welsh route was found to be impossible. All the Severn crossings and boats were guarded by the Parliamentary militia, which had put up posters everywhere offering the sum £1000 to anybody who could find the Prince. After several weeks of unsuccessful escape attempts Charles returned to the Boscobel estate, where he and a companion hid in a now famous oak tree (today's is a descendant) while Parliamentary soldiers searched Boscobel House. Finally Charles, now dressed as servant to a yeoman's daughter called Jane Lane, riding pillion (two on one horse) as was the norm for servant and mistress, tried to reach the coast somewhere. After several mishaps Charles arrived on 13 October at Brighthelmstone (Brighton). It was from Hove that he eventually managed to embark on a boat and escape to France. Later, after the young Prince was restored as Charles II in the year 1660, Jane Lane was rewarded with a watch, a jewel worth £1000 and a yearly pension of an equal amount.

7. The Prince of Wales, later Regent and King George IV, as the leader of fashion among the dandies, was well known to dress up in the most outrageous costumes.

8. The first iron bridge spans the Severn still. The Ironbridge Museum is a large working museum featuring the first steps in Britain's industrialisation. Also on the site is the Museum of Iron.

9. The Maltings

10. It had long been converted into offices and a shops when it was known as Talbot Chambers. It burnt down in February 1985.

Selective Bibliography

Local History

Champion Bill, Everyday Life in Tudor Shrewsbury, Shropshire Books, 1994

Cromarty Dorothy, Everyday Life in Medieval Shrewsbury, Shropshire Books, 1991

Fletcher J M J, Mrs. Wightman of Shrewsbury, Longmans & Co., London 1906

Owen and Blakeway, A History of Shrewsbury, Vol. I, 1825

Priestley E J, The Battle of Shrewsbury 1403, Shrewsbury and Atcham Bourough Council, 1979

Priestley E J, An Illustrated History of Shrewsbury, Shrewsbury and Atcham Borough Council, 1989

Trinder Barrie, A History of Shropshire, Phillimore, 1983

Trinder Barrie, ed., Victorian Shrewsbury (Studies in the History of a County Town by the Victorian Shrewsbury Research Group) Shropshire Libraries, 1984

Trumper David, The Twentieth Century Shrewsbury

Tudor Genevieve, ed., Shropshire Century Speaks, Shropshire Books, BBC

Video of Shrewsbury

Shrewsbury Chronicle

Eddows Journal

Shropshire Magazine

General History

Anglo-Saxon Chronicle, Brewer, Cambridge 1983

Peter J Bowler, Charles Darwin, The Man and His Influence, Blackwells, Oxford 1990

Roy Burrell, The Romans, Oxford Univ. Press, 1991

Cobbett, Rural Rides, ed. By George Woodcock, Penguin, (1967)

Peter Connolly, The Roman Army, Macdonald Educational, 1975

Daniel Defoe, A Tour thro' the Whole Island of Great Britain, 1724

John Davies, A History of Wales, first published by Allen Lane, The Penguin Press, 1990

Christopher Duffy, Siege Warfare, Routledge and Kegan, 1979

Edna Healey, Emma Darwin, Headline Book Publishing, London, 2001.

Malcolm Hebron, The Medieval Siege, Clarendon Press, 1997

Bert S Hall, Weapons and Warfare in Renaissance Europe, John Hopkins University Press, Baltimore and London, 1997

C. Hill, The World Turned Upside Down, Penguin Books Ltd, London, 1972.

J L Kirby, Henry IV of England, Constable, London, 1970

Samuel Richardson, Pamela, Penguin Books, 1985 (first published 1740)

Nigel Saul, Richard II, Yale University Press, 1997

Alan Sorrell, Roman Towns in Britain, Batsford, London 1976

Stanley Wells and Gary Taylor, William Shakespeare, The Complete Works, Clarendon Press, Oxford, 1988

P. Ziegler, The Black Death, Penguin Books Ltd., 1969

Shrewsbury Museum & Art Gallery

Shrewsbury Museum and Art Gallery, housed in Rowley's House, contains extensive collections that celebrate Shropshire's variety. These include bronze age metal work and log-boats, artifacts from the Roman city of Viriconium and ceramics produced during the Industrial Revolution in Ironbridge. A medieval section and costumes throughout the ages are also on display.